EXTRAORDINARY PEOPLE

A Semi-Comprehensive Guide to Some of the World's Most Fascinating Individuals

WRITTEN BY
MICHAEL HEARST

ILLUSTRATED BY
AARON SCAMIHORN

chronicle books·san francisco

Library of Congress Cataloging-in-Publication Data available.

ISBN 978-1-4521-2709-5

Manufactured in China.

Design by Aaron Scamihorn & Ryan Hayes.
Typeset in Whitney.

10 9 8 7 6 5 4 3 2 1

Chronicle Books LLC
680 Second Street
San Francisco, CA 94107

Chronicle Books—we see things differently.
Become part of our community at www.chroniclekids.com.

To Kelly, extraordinary with her love
and support for so many years.

CONTENTS

THERE ARE MANY, MANY EXTRAORDINARY PEOPLE OUT THERE. HERE ARE THE PEOPLE I HAVE CHOSEN FOR THIS BOOK.

Okay, so if you count the names after the ampersands, there are actually fifty-two people on this list. (By the way, the symbol "&" is called an ampersand; it means "and." But you probably already knew that, since you're extraordinary.)

Well, it could be any number of traits or qualities, or even circumstances . . . or a combination thereof. Some of the obvious labels might include "Scientist," "Daredevil," and "Humanitarian." But what about somebody who is extraordinary because he survived a near-death experience? Or because she overcame discrimination? (An "Overcomer"?) With this in mind, I've come up with an easy-to-read chart . . .

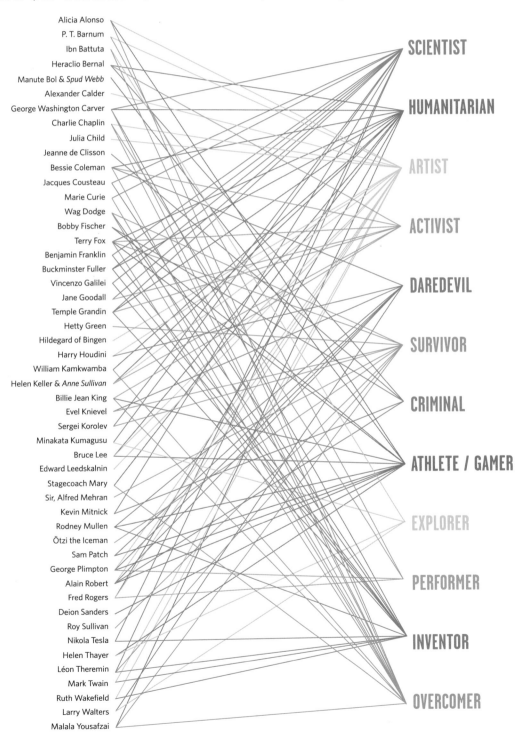

Alicia Alonso
P. T. Barnum
Ibn Battuta
Heraclio Bernal
Manute Bol & *Spud Webb*
Alexander Calder
George Washington Carver
Charlie Chaplin
Julia Child
Jeanne de Clisson
Bessie Coleman
Jacques Cousteau
Marie Curie
Wag Dodge
Bobby Fischer
Terry Fox
Benjamin Franklin
Buckminster Fuller
Vincenzo Galilei
Jane Goodall
Temple Grandin
Hetty Green
Hildegard of Bingen
Harry Houdini
William Kamkwamba
Helen Keller & *Anne Sullivan*
Billie Jean King
Evel Knievel
Sergei Korolev
Minakata Kumagusu
Bruce Lee
Edward Leedskalnin
Stagecoach Mary
Sir, Alfred Mehran
Kevin Mitnick
Rodney Mullen
Ötzi the Iceman
Sam Patch
George Plimpton
Alain Robert
Fred Rogers
Deion Sanders
Roy Sullivan
Nikola Tesla
Helen Thayer
Léon Theremin
Mark Twain
Ruth Wakefield
Larry Walters
Malala Yousafzai

SCIENTIST
HUMANITARIAN
ARTIST
ACTIVIST
DAREDEVIL
SURVIVOR
CRIMINAL
ATHLETE / GAMER
EXPLORER
PERFORMER
INVENTOR
OVERCOMER

A WORD FROM THE AUTHOR

CHANCES ARE, YOU HAVE SOME QUESTIONS ABOUT THIS BOOK. PERHAPS THEY ARE:

1. Why are all these people together in the same book?

2. What gives Michael Hearst the authority to pick and choose who goes in this book?

3. How did Michael find out about these people?

4. Why am I not in this book?

ANSWERS:

1. All of these people are extraordinary. "Extraordinary" means *beyond ordinary*. Some are daredevils, some are geniuses, some are eccentrics, some are humanitarians, some are heroes, and some are criminals. ("Extraordinary" is not necessarily the same as "role model.")

2. My publisher said I could. So there.

3. Research, and lots of it. Sometimes on the Internet, sometimes in my local library. (Libraries are awesome. You should spend more time in yours. Tell them I said hi.) Sometimes I would remember an article I'd read in the newspaper about somebody who did something extraordinary. Other times I'd simply recall a person whom I loved learning about when I was younger. But even with those particular people, there was always something new to learn. As it turned out, the more I researched, the more fun it was to write this book.

4. Because I haven't heard of you yet. If you would like to convince me of how extraordinary you are, you may write to me at:

Michael Hearst
c/o Chronicle Children's Books
680 Second Street
San Francisco, CA 94107

YOURS, MICHAEL HEARST

P.S. "Extraordinary" is sort of a funny word, isn't it? It breaks down into two words: "extra" and "ordinary." If you think about it, it seems like the word "extraordinary" should mean *very* ordinary. Twice as ordinary. Perhaps a better word would be "abovordinary," (above-ordinary). In fact, I hereby declare "abovordinary" a word. If you want to refer to this book as "Abovordinary People," I have no problem with that.

ALICIA ALONSO

BORN IN HAVANA, CUBA • 1921–

Viva Alicia Alonso, the Cuban *prima ballerina assoluta*! She not only helped put Cuba and America on the world ballet map, but she also heroically did it while facing a lifelong struggle with near-blindness.

Alonso's full birth name (ready for this?) was Alicia Ernestina de la Caridad del Cobre Martínez y del Hoyo, but her friends and family simply called her Unga. At a very early age, she showed great interest in music and dance—her mother could entertain her simply by playing records on the phonograph and twirling a scarf. By the time Alicia was eight, she was studying at the Sociedad Pro-Arte Músical in Havana under Bolshoi ballerina Sophie Fedorova. A year later she performed publicly for the first time in Tchaikovsky's *Sleeping Beauty*.

She progressed rapidly, and at the age of sixteen, she married fellow dancer Fernando Alonso. The couple moved to New York City, where she continued studying at the School of American Ballet.

Unfortunately, around this time she also began to lose her vision due to a detached retina. She underwent three surgeries to repair her eyes, and was ordered by doctors to stay in bed for an entire year! She was told to rest as motionless as possible, and was not allowed to laugh, cry, or even chew too hard. Alonso continued to practice ballet in her head, pointing and stretching her feet to keep them active. After the year was over, the doctors declared that the surgery had been *unsuccessful* and she would never have peripheral vision. Oy!

Defying her doctors' orders, the strong-willed Alonso began dancing again. She would often count her steps and use lights to help determine her location onstage. And even with these setbacks, she was amazing! Her stardom rose with roles in *Giselle* and *Swan Lake*, and soon she was named principal dancer of the American Ballet.

She returned to Cuba in 1948, hoping to develop ballet in her homeland, and started the Alicia Alonso Ballet Company. Although her company was a success with audiences everywhere, there was very little money to be made. When Fidel Castro took power of Cuba in 1959, he increased funding to the arts. Alicia received $200,000 for her company. Castro, however, also asked that she change the name to Ballet Nacional de Cuba.

Because of her new affiliation to the communist government, Alicia fell out of grace with many of her American fans. Regardless, she persevered throughout Europe, Canada, and, of course, Cuba. Alicia Alonso continues to direct her ballet company. She is in her nineties and almost entirely blind.

BUT WHAT IS A PRIMA BALLERINA ASSOLUTA?

"Prima ballerina assoluta" is a title given to the most exceptional female ballet dancers. It is a very rare honor. In other words, Alicia Alonso is *extraordinary*!

★ FIDEL CASTRO ★

Thanks to Cuban leader Fidel Castro, Alicia Alonso was able to support her ballet company. However, this is also the reason she disappeared from the American artistic scene.

CUBA

P. T. BARNUM

BORN IN BETHEL, CT • DIED IN BRIDGEPORT, CT • 1810–1891

Phineas Taylor Barnum once said, "Whatever you do, do with all your might. Work at it if necessary early and late, in season and out of season, not leaving a stone unturned, and never deferring for a single hour that which can be done just as well *now*." And with this drive, P. T. Barnum became the best-known showman of his time. He tirelessly promoted human curiosities, music concerts, and animal attractions.

Barnum's American Museum in New York City featured strange and educational items such as an aquarium, taxidermy exhibits, wax figures, paintings, and memorabilia. Ultimately, he joined his rival James A. Bailey to create the Barnum & Bailey Circus, the first traveling three-ring show. And it was not just *any* show. It was "The Greatest Show on Earth." Or so they claim.

SOME OF P. T. BARNUM'S SPECTACULAR SPECTACLES

- General Tom Thumb, "The Smallest Man in the World." At 3 feet 4 inches (1 metre) tall, Charles Stratton (a.k.a. Tom Thumb) traveled the world with Barnum, appearing before Queen Victoria in Britain and Abraham Lincoln at the White House.

- Jenny Lind, an opera singer also known as the "Swedish Nightingale."
- Chang and Eng, conjoined twins who often bickered with each other—as well as with Barnum.
- Josephine Clofullia, a Swiss bearded woman.

JENNY LIND

CHANG AND ENG

JOSEPHINE CLOFULLIA

WHICH ONE OF THESE IS NOT TRUE?

1. Barnum would occasionally create hoaxes to help promote his attractions.
2. Barnum served as a Connecticut legislator and as mayor of Bridgeport.
3. Barnum wrote several books including his hugely successful autobiography, *The Life of P. T. Barnum*.
4. Barnum's last words were, "How were the receipts today at Madison Square Garden?"
5. His diet consisted of nothing more than animal crackers and milk.

Answers: 1. T (My favorite being the Feejee Mermaid, which had the head of a monkey and the tail of a fish. Monkfish?); 2. T; 3. T; 4. T; 5. F (but sounds delicious!).

IBN BATTUTA

BORN IN TANGIER, MOROCCO • DIED IN MOROCCO • 1304–1377

Road trip! At the age of twenty-one, Ibn Battuta said good-bye to his friends and family in Morocco and set off on a journey that would last twenty-four years!

Of course there weren't many roads for a road trip in the 1300s; nor were there airplanes or frequent flyer miles for that matter. Instead, Battuta traveled on camel, boat, and foot, covering approximately 75,000 miles (120,700 kilometres), and visiting just about the entire known Islamic world, and then some.

His journey began with a *hajj* (or pilgrimage) to Mecca, the holiest city in the Islamic world. The voyage, which took sixteen months, covered 3,000 miles (4,828 kilometres) of the northern edge of Africa.

After reaching Mecca and exploring much of the Middle East, Battuta decided he wanted more. He headed north to what is now Iraq and Iran, and then back down the Red Sea to Tanzania and the Swahili Coast. In 1332, he headed up to India, where he was welcomed by the sultan of Delhi and was offered a job as a judge (which, incidentally, happened to be his family's trade back in Morocco).

Battuta stayed in India for eight years, but then, perhaps with itchy feet, headed for China. In 1349, he finally returned home, where he learned that his father had died fifteen years earlier, and his mother had passed away just a few months before his arrival.

Unable to stay put, Battuta set out once again, this time through Spain to regions of Morocco he had not yet explored, and then to the African kingdom of Mali and the city of Timbuktu. In 1354, he returned to Morocco for good, where we can only hope he threw out his shoes and took a hot bath.

CARAVAN!

Battuta would occasionally team up with caravans (groups of people traveling together, often on trade routes) to avoid the risk of being attacked by bandits. Plus it no doubt made traveling a little less lonely.

BUT HOW DO WE KNOW ALL THIS?

Not only was Ibn Battuta an extraordinary explorer, but he was also extraordinary at recounting his adventures. Upon Battuta's return to Morocco, Sultan Abu Inan Faris was so impressed that he had Battuta dictate his stories into a book known as the *Rihla* ("The Journey").

DURING HIS TRAVELS, IBN BATTUTA:

1. married several women.
2. survived a shipwreck while on a visit to China.
3. covered three times as much distance as Marco Polo.
4. covered enough miles to equal three trips around Earth at the equator!
5. stopped for lunch at the food court in the Ibn Battuta Mall in Dubai. (Okay, I made the last one up. The mall was only recently built.)

HERACLIO BERNAL

Heraclio Bernal, the "Thunderbolt of Sinaloa," was a famous (or perhaps infamous) *bandito* from the Sinaloa region of Mexico. In case it's not clear, "bandito" is Spanish for "bandit." In other words, he was an outlaw! But Bernal was a generous outlaw, more like Robin Hood, stealing from the rich and then giving to the poor, in his case laid-off mine workers and needy pueblo dwellers. He fought for social causes, in particular the emancipation of Mexican workers.

Not that this makes what Bernal did any less of a crime, especially in the eyes of Mexican President Porfirio Díaz, who put a ten-thousand-peso bounty on Bernal's head. But the Thunderbolt of Sinaloa persisted along with a band of as many as one hundred *pistoleros* (gunmen) who followed him on his raids of stagecoaches, armories, and silver mines.

Although Bernal and his posse managed to evade capture for at least ten years, keeping a hideout in the remote mountains of Durango, the law finally caught up with him. There are many stories about his death, one being that his close friend, Crispin Garcia, who was standing guard at a hideout cave, actually shot Bernal several times so that he could collect the bounty. According to others, Bernal was surrounded by government forces and killed near the mines of Nuestra Senora. Whatever the case may be, Heraclio Bernal certainly lives on in Mexican lore.

SING A SONG

Heraclio Bernal is the subject of countless Mexican *corridos*, or folk songs, typically praising him as a hero. *"Que rechulo era Bernal, en su caballo retinto, con su pistola en la manopeleando con treinta y cinco."* ("How beautiful was Bernal, on his black horse, with pistol in hand, fighting against thirty-five.")

A BRAVE GRINGO

Legend has it that on one occasion, Bernal and his gang ambushed a stagecoach traveling from Mazatlán to Culiacán. A "tall blond" man and his wife courageously fought back, but ultimately lost the battle and were forced out of the carriage. After looting their carriage for valuables, Bernal's troops asked what to do with the couple. Bernal ordered them to be left alone, saying, "A brave gringo is respected, not killed." He then treated their injuries and escorted them to the outskirts of Culiacán so they could avoid being assaulted again.

MANUTE BOL

Taller and ganglier than you can possibly imagine, Manute Bol ran the NBA courts from 1985 to 1995, playing for the Washington Bullets, the Golden State Warriors, the Philadelphia 76ers, and the Miami Heat.

Just how tall was he? He was 7 feet 7 inches (2.3 metres)—pretty darn tall! And according to *Sports Illustrated*, he could reach a whopping 10 feet (3 metres) with his arms in the air. In other words, the dude could dunk the ball just by standing on his tiptoes! His strong suit, however, was in blocking—he was considered one of the best shot blockers in the sport.

But Bol's extraordinary existence extended beyond just his height and skills with basketball. He was an activist and humanitarian, in particular for his home nation of Sudan. Bol was born to the Dinka tribe; the name "Manute" means "special blessing." And he was indeed a blessing to the people of Sudan. During and after his NBA career, he made frequent trips home, visiting refugee camps and donating the vast majority of his money to various Sudanese refugee causes.

Bol was always treated like royalty during his visits. In fact, in 2001 the Sudanese government offered him a position as minister of sport, but he turned it down because it would have required him to convert from Christianity to Islam.

In 2001 Bol established the Ring True Foundation to continue fund-raising for Sudanese refugees and to help young African student-athletes find places in American schools. Sadly, he passed away in 2010 from complications of a rare skin condition.

THE GREATEST OF GREAT-GRANDFATHERS

Manute Bol's tribe, the Dinka, are some of the tallest people in the world. Bol's father was 6 feet 8 inches (2 metres), his mother 6 feet 10 inches (2.1 metres), and allegedly his great-grandfather was a colossal 7 feet 10 inches (2.4 metres)!

A WORD FROM CHARLIE

Basketball great Charles Barkley once said, "If everyone in the world was a Manute Bol, it's a world I'd want to live in. He's smart. He reads *The New York Times*. He knows what's going on in a lot of subjects. He's not one of these just-basketball guys."

HEADS UP!

In the 1990s, Manute Bol visited the Pentagon and Congress several times to warn them about the rising threat of Islamic fundamentalism, specifically about Osama bin Laden, who had been given a safe haven by the Sudanese government.

SPUD WEBB

We may as well add Spud Webb to this page. At 5 feet 7 inches (1.7 metres), he was one of the shortest players in the NBA. But what made him *extra*-extraordinary was the fact that he could dunk! In fact, he won the NBA Slam Dunk Contest in 1986 against his teammate, 7-foot-8-inch (2.2-metre) defending dunk champion Dominique Wilkins! In 1985 Webb and Bol were on the same semipro team after college, the Rhode Island Gulls.

GEORGE WASHINGTON CARVER

BORN IN DIAMOND, MO • DIED IN TUSKEGEE, AL • 1864–1943

Perhaps you already know that George Washington Carver invented peanut butter. But did you know that he also came up with more than three hundred other uses for peanuts? Three hundred! Not to mention hundreds of uses for sweet potatoes, pecans, and soybeans. To name just a few: shoe polish, meat tenderizer, instant coffee, milk, glue, mayonnaise, shampoo, fabric dyes, wallboard, candies, and wood fillers. I could go on and on. Okay, I will! Insulating boards, molasses feed, starch, printing ink, synthetic rubber, talcum powder, shaving cream, paper, fuel briquettes, and even chili sauce!

Carver was born into slavery, but his thirst for knowledge was insatiable, and he excelled in his studies. With the conclusion of the Civil War and the end of slavery, he was able to attend a series of schools and receive a high school diploma. Despite much racial discrimination, Carver became the first black student to attend Iowa State, where he ultimately received a master's degree. He went on to become a world-renowned agricultural scientist.

After Carver graduated, the Tuskegee Institute invited him to head its Agriculture Department. He taught there for forty-seven years, during which time he became a household name, thanks to his numerous inventions and advancements to farming, which included techniques to improve soils and the advocating of crop rotation. He was praised by such luminaries as Booker T. Washington and Theodore Roosevelt. I also praise him, because I love peanut butter. Preferably chunky.

TRADED FOR A HORSE

A week after his birth, George was kidnapped along with his mother and sister by slave raiders. Although his mother and sister were never found, little George was traded back to his owners for a racehorse.

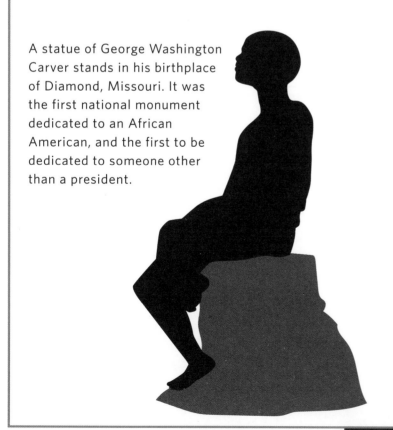

A statue of George Washington Carver stands in his birthplace of Diamond, Missouri. It was the first national monument dedicated to an African American, and the first to be dedicated to someone other than a president.

A FEW OF GEORGE WASHINGTON CARVER'S PEANUT PRODUCTS

SHOE POLISH

SHAMPOO

CANDY

MILK

FUEL BRIQUETTES

CHARLIE CHAPLIN

BORN IN LONDON, ENGLAND • DIED IN VEVEY, SWITZERLAND • 1889–1977

Long before movies like *Avatar* and *Star Wars*, before Technicolor and even "talkies" (films with sound), British actor and comedian Charlie Chaplin waddled onto the silver screen with his bowler hat and bamboo cane, bringing laughs to millions. And not only did he star in more than eighty films, but he also wrote, directed, produced, edited, and even scored most of them (that is, when sound was finally added to films).

Charlie Chaplin became one of the most recognized and highest paid actors of his time, as well as one of the most important figures in the history of film. But if there ever were a rags-to-riches story, it belongs to Chaplin.

Born to theater-performer parents in London, Charlie grew up dreaming of a career on stage. Sadly, his parents separated when he was just three, and a few years later his mother was admitted to an asylum. Charlie and his brothers were forced to fend for themselves, constantly battling poverty and difficult times. Thanks to his older brother, Sydney, who had begun working on the stage, Charlie was also given a chance to act at the age of thirteen.

When he was nineteen, Charlie joined a pantomime vaudeville group that toured the United States. During the tour, a representative from the Keystone film company noticed his incredible talents, and offered him a yearly contract for $150 a week—a hefty income for that time.

Over the next several years he appeared in dozens of films for Keystone, to great success. In 1915 Chaplin switched to the Essanay Company, which would pay him $1,250 a week. There he quickly became a megastar with a character he had developed called "The Little Tramp," an iconic man with a bowler hat, cane, and small mustache. Now things were really taking off.

At the age of twenty-six, Chaplin signed a contract with the Mutual Film Corporation for $670,000 a year, making him one of the highest paid people in the world! But Chaplin ultimately wanted to be his own boss, so in 1919, along with movie stars Mary Pickford and Douglas Fairbanks, and director D. W. Griffith, he started his own company called United Artists.

Chaplin's hits, such as *Modern Times*, *The Kid*, and *City Lights*, are films that are forever studied and revered by actors and moviemakers around the world. One of his final productions, *The Great Dictator*, made fun of Hitler and Mussolini. The film was released during a sensitive time for the United States, just before our involvement with World War II. Because of this, Chaplin became a target of right-wing conservatives who wanted to kick him out of the country. On one particular trip to England, he was told that he would not be allowed back into the United States without proving his "moral worth."

Chaplin decided to live in Europe for the rest of his life. He did, however, return to the United States in 1972 to receive an honorary Oscar "for the incalculable effect he has had in making motion pictures the art form of this century." At the Academy Awards ceremony, he received a twelve-minute standing ovation—the longest in the history of the Oscars.

IN WHAT SOUNDS LIKE A SCENE FROM ONE OF HIS MOVIES . . .

Soon after Charlie Chaplin passed away in Switzerland, thieves dug up his coffin and demanded $400,000 for its return. The men were eventually arrested and Chaplin's body was recovered. His body is now buried in a vault surrounded by cement.

RUMOR HAS IT

Charlie Chaplin once entered a Charlie Chaplin look-alike contest . . . and came in third.

MAESTRO

After finishing his final film, in 1967, Charlie Chaplin went back and composed music for many of his earlier silent films.

THAT'S SIR TO YOU
Queen Elizabeth II knighted Chaplin in 1975. Sir Charlie Chaplin!

JULIA CHILD

Before Julia Child, food in America was boring! Not really. But thanks to an encyclopedic cookbook called *Mastering the Art of French Cooking*, published in 1961, things certainly changed for the better. Child, who was just one of the three authors (the other two being French), was specifically brought on board to help make the book more appealing to Americans. And she did just that, proving to home cooks across the United States that making an omelet really wasn't so difficult.

But the fun didn't stop there. Six-foot-two-inch-(2-metre-)tall Child and her enthusiastically warbly voice went on to host a television series called *The French Chef*. The show (one of the first cooking shows on television) lasted ten years, bringing with it a sense of ease to making such dishes as beef bourguignon and zucchini (courgette) au gratin. It also turned her into a household name. Over the next several decades she went on to publish a multitude of books and host several other television shows.

Today Child's legacy lives on in the form of deliciousness around the world, albeit with a little extra butter and cream. As she once said, "The only time to eat diet food is while you're waiting for the steak to cook."

Before Child wrote cookbooks, she worked as a research assistant for the Secret Intelligence division at the Office of Strategic Services (OSS), where she cataloged highly classified communications for the OSS's secret stations in Asia. In other words, Julia Child was a spy!

HOOP DREAMS

Julia Child wore a size 12 (UK 10) shoe, and played basketball at Smith College in Massachusetts.

INCIDENTALLY

- *Mastering the Art of French Cooking* was initially rejected by the publisher Houghton Mifflin because they thought it was too much like an encyclopedia. Of course, that was the point! The book was eventually published by Knopf, and quickly became a bestseller.
- Julia Child died of natural causes two days before her ninety-second birthday. Her final meal was a bowl of French onion soup.
- French onion soup in France is simply called "onion soup."

JEANNE DE CLISSON

BIRTHPLACE UNKNOWN • DIED IN HENNEBONT, FRANCE • 1300–1359

Yes, women can be pirates, too! Jeanne de Clisson, also known as the "Lioness of Brittany," spent thirteen years of her life sailing the English Channel, hunting down French ships. When she found them, she would destroy them, killing the men on board . . . but sparing just a few, to make sure her message got back to the French king.

Born Jeanne-Louise de Belleville, at the age of thirty she married a wealthy nobleman, Olivier III de Clisson, who owned a castle and large amounts of land around Nantes, France. In 1342, Olivier joined Breton forces to help defend Brittany from the English. Unfortunately, just a year later, he was accused of treason and sentenced to death by King Philip VI. Jeanne was beyond outraged,

and swore revenge upon the French king. She sold off her husband's land and bought three warships, which she had painted black and the sails dyed red.

For more than a decade, the Lioness of Brittany hunted French ships, beheading the sailors and throwing the bodies overboard. Even after the king died in 1350, Jeanne continued her piracy, fighting for England to keep the Channel free from French warships.

Eventually, in 1356, Jeanne hung up her pirate hat and settled down with a new husband, Sir Walter Bentley. The Lioness of Brittany had been feared by many and praised by many others, and without a doubt, had proved to King Philip VI that he had messed with the wrong gal.

IT HAS BEEN SAID . . .

. . . that the ghost of Jeanne de Clisson makes an occasional appearance in the halls of Château de Clisson. Apparently revenge on the king was not enough to settle the Lioness of Brittany's anguished soul.

IT HAS ALSO BEEN SAID . . .

. . . that September 19 is International Talk Like a Pirate Day. *À l'abordage!*

The skull and crossbones flag wasn't used by Jean. It's more of an 18th century pirate thing. Nonetheless, it looks good in this drawing, don't you think?

Jeanne de Clisson sailed "The Black Fleet" through the English Channel.

BESSIE COLEMAN

Bessie Coleman loved to read about World War I airplane pilots. She, too, wanted to fly. Unfortunately, getting a pilot's license was not so easy for a woman in 1918, especially an African American woman. Flying schools in the United States denied her entry; however, Coleman had heard that women could learn to fly in France. So she did exactly what any extraordinary African American woman in the early 20th century would have done: She learned French and moved to Paris!

It took her seven months of training, mostly in clunky biplanes. In fact, she witnessed a fellow student crash and die, which was a terrible shock. But she persisted, and in 1921, she became the first black woman to receive a pilot's license.

When Coleman returned to America, she was met by reporters and cheering fans. She became a stunt pilot, barnstorming at numerous air shows specializing in aerial tricks and parachuting. (Incidentally, she would turn down events where African Americans were not allowed.) She was a hero to women and men all over, and became known affectionately as "Queen Bess."

Unfortunately, Queen Bess took her final flight in 1926, when she was just thirty-four. It was the day before a big air show in Florida, and she was practicing with a recently purchased airplane that was perhaps not mechanically fit. High above the ground, a loose wrench slipped into the control gears, and the plane took a sharp dive. Coleman had not been wearing her seat belt, and was thrown from the plane. She fell 3,500 feet (1.1 kilometres) to her death.

And while the ending to this story is quite sad, we should remember Queen Bess for her achievements: her contributions to racial and gender equality, as well as her inspiration in the form of adventure, positive attitude, and determination to succeed.

BARNSTORMING

Barnstorming was a popular form of entertainment back in the 1920s, in which pilots flew from one farm field to another and performed airplane stunts, such as loop-the-loops and wing walking. Incidentally, the term "barnstorming" comes from politics. Candidates would travel the countryside making speeches in barns!

LAND LEGS

Bessie Coleman was part African American and part Cherokee. She had twelve brothers and sisters, and grew up at a time of strong racial tension. As children, she and her siblings had to walk a whopping 4 miles (6.4 kilometres) each day to get to their single-room school, segregated for black children.

A DANGEROUS PROFESSION

In 1923 Coleman had a less tragic plane crash while taking off from a new fairground in Los Angeles. She broke a leg and several ribs, but mostly she felt bad that she had disappointed her fans.

JACQUES COUSTEAU

BORN IN SAINT-ANDRÉ-DE-CUBZAC, FRANCE • DIED IN PARIS, FRANCE • 1910–1997

If there ever was an ambassador of the sea, it was Jacques Cousteau. He spent decades of his life traveling, exploring the oceans. Along the way, he wrote more than fifty books, made dozens of documentary films, and even helped invent the Aqua-Lung, a breathing device for scuba divers. But how did it all start?

As a young man, Cousteau was in a bad car accident, sustaining multiple injuries. As part of his rehabilitation, he began swimming every day in the Mediterranean Sea. At some point, a friend lent him a pair of goggles, which opened his eyes to an underwater world!

In the 1940s, he began documenting his explorations in the form of writing, but quickly realized how great it would be if he could film all the amazing things he saw. And with that, Cousteau helped develop a waterproof camera—a camera that could withstand the great pressures of the deep sea.

On one of the first expeditions with his new camera, he explored a 2,200-year-old shipwreck. Many say it marked the beginning of "underwater archaeology." Of course, these endeavors can get quite expensive, and for a while Cousteau struggled with money. But then, thanks to the success of several books and films, he was able to continue financing his exploration and research.

Eventually Cousteau was approached by ABC television to produce a series, *The Undersea World of Jacques Cousteau*, which ran for nine seasons. Millions of viewers were able to travel (so to speak) with him on his journey to reveal the mysteries of the underwater world. During this time, he realized how much of the oceans were being destroyed by pollution from humans, and thus started the Cousteau Society to raise awareness and protect ocean wildlife.

Although Cousteau is no longer with us, his foundation continues to explore, observe, and help people understand the importance and "fragility of life on our Water Planet."

CORKED

While exploring a 2,000-year-old shipwreck, Cousteau and his team found several sealed wine jars. They tried the wine, but they didn't like it.

EVER HEARD OF SCUBA?

The Aqua-Lung, which Cousteau invented with his friend Émile Gagnan, was the first "self-contained underwater breathing apparatus." Hey, just out of curiosity, what happens if you take the first letter of each of those words and put them together?

DID YOU KNOW?

Only 5 percent of the oceans have been explored. In fact, the amount of money we've spent on exploration of the sea is just a tiny fraction of what we've spent to explore outer space.

THE CALYPSO

Jacques Cousteau's renowned research vessel, *Calypso*, was a former British minesweeper. It served Cousteau and his team until 1996, when it was accidentally struck by a barge in Singapore harbor, and sank.

MARIE CURIE

BORN IN WARSAW, POLAND • DIED IN PASSY, FRANCE • 1867–1934

Marie Curie was curious about the invisible rays coming from a metal called uranium. With her husband, Pierre, she went about the process of separating uranium from rocks so that she could better understand how "radiation," as she called it, worked. Along the way, she discovered a couple of other radioactive metals; one she named "polonium" after her home country of Poland, and the other "radium," because . . . well, it sounded like the word "radiation."

In 1903 the Curies were awarded the Nobel Prize in Physics for their work. Marie was the first Polish person and the first woman to win the prize! Pierre became a professor at the University of Paris, and Marie ran the lab. Sadly, one day Pierre slipped in front of his horse-drawn wagon and was killed instantly. Marie, with her chin up, took over his classes, becoming the first woman professor at the university. In 1911 she won a second Nobel Prize, this time for her work in chemistry.

Scientists ultimately realized how dangerous radiation could be, but it was too late for Marie. She was beginning to go blind, and had also developed a blood disease from the invisible rays. She died in 1934.

In 1995 Marie continued to break ground when her remains were transferred to the Panthéon in Paris—a memorial dedicated to France's greatest men!

STILL RADIOACTIVE

Well, I guess *somebody* had to research radiation! And as it turns out, it's very useful for many things—X-ray machines, getting rid of cancer, generating electricity, and, of course, evil weapons. To this day Marie Curie's notebooks are still locked away because they're too radioactive to handle!

ALL IN THE FAMILY

The Curies' daughter Irène Joliot-Curie and her husband, Frédéric Joliot-Curie, were also physicists involved in the study of radioactivity. They too were awarded Nobel Prizes for their work.

ODE TO MARIE

Madame Curie, your discovery
Of radium was quite wise.
For that they have bestowed on thee—
The noblest Nobel Prize.

Madame Curie, so extraordinary.
In the world you've left your mark.
A museum should display your notes,
Even if they glow in the dark.

HERE COMES THE X-RAY TRUCK!

During World War I, Curie drove a truck around the battlefields. The truck contained an X-ray machine used to treat wounded soldiers.

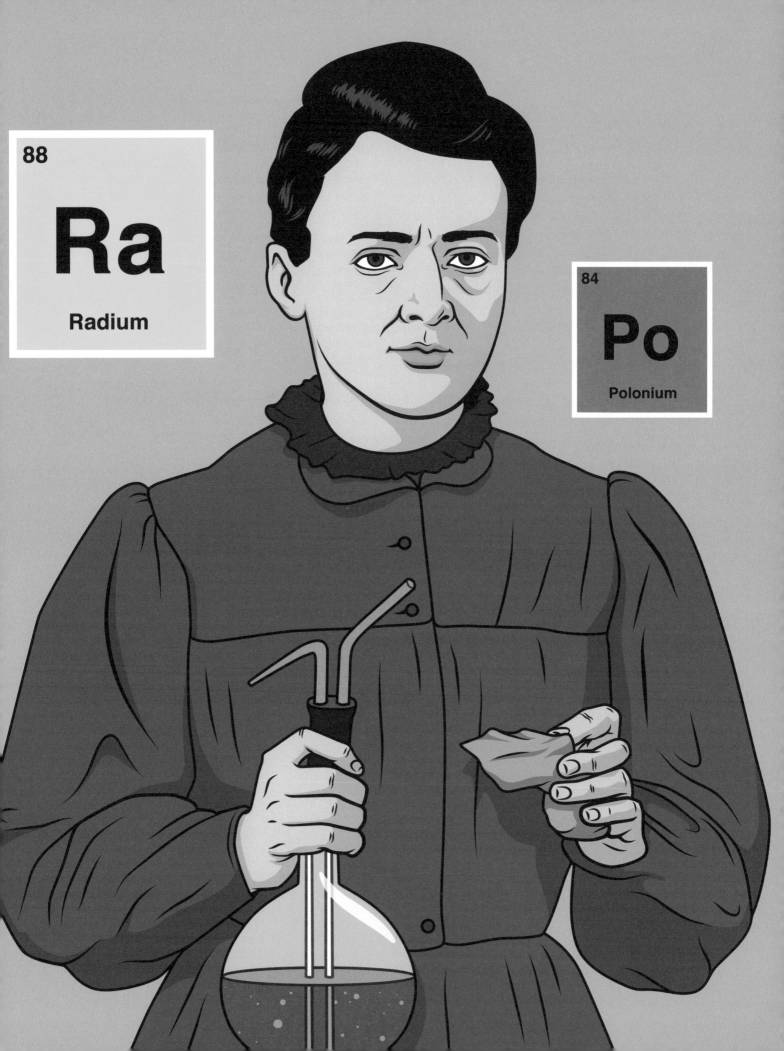

WAG DODGE

BORN IN HIAWATHA, MI • DIED IN MISSOULA, MT • 1915–1955

First off, it should be pointed out that Wag Dodge has one of the coolest names known to mankind. Second, not much is known about Wag Dodge except for what took place on August 5, 1949. But what *did* take place is pretty darn astonishing.

Wag Dodge was the chief for a crew of fifteen smoke jumpers (firefighters who parachute from airplanes to forest fires). They had been called in to combat a raging fire in the Helena National Forest, which had been started by lightning.

Dodge and his crew jumped from a C-47 aircraft into an area known as Mann Gulch. Almost immediately they realized the intensity of the fire, which burned at temperatures of thousands of degrees and traveled at 600 feet (183 metres) per minute. Because of strong winds and the steep incline of the gulch, the fire suddenly began moving up the grasses toward the smoke jumpers at an alarming rate. The men began to retreat to the ridge as quickly as possible, but the wall of flames was catching up with them.

Dodge suddenly came up with a brilliant idea: He stopped, took a match from his pocket, and lit a fire at his feet, burning the grasses around him. He yelled to his crew, instructing them to join him in his burned-out circle. The men, likely thinking he was crazy, stuck with their instincts to get out of the gulch as quickly as possible.

Dodge crouched in the middle of his burned-out section of grass and waited for the fire to pass. Of the fifteen men, the fire claimed the lives of thirteen. Wag Dodge walked away unharmed.

ESCAPE FIRE

Dodge thought outside the box, and in the heat of the moment (pun intended) he came up with what is known today as an "escape fire."

UPHILL BATTLE?

Fire may be one of the few things in nature that can travel uphill faster than downhill.

SIDE NOTE

On the flight to Mann Gulch, the winds were so strong and turbulent that one smoke jumper became airsick. He decided not to jump, and instead returned with the airplane back to the base.

OUTSIDE THE BOX

Being able to recognize a good idea and implement it can be just as important as the idea itself. Although Dodge spent the remainder of his life unsure where his moment of intuitive brilliance had come from, the story has become an emblem for visionary thinking, the ability to think beyond the obvious. Dodge did something that none of the other men did: Instead of running away from the fire, he stopped and figured out a way to keep the fire from reaching him.

P.S. Wag is short for Wagner. Wagner Dodge! That's still one of the coolest names ever.

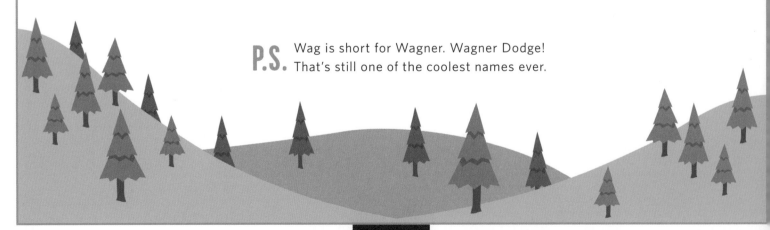

BOBBY FISCHER

Bobby Fischer was just six when his sister bought him a chess set from the candy store below their Brooklyn apartment. He was instantly hooked. Perhaps too hooked—he couldn't stop playing! His mother tried to persuade him to find other interests, but the chess set kept coming out . . . even at the dinner table.

By the time he was fourteen, Bobby was so good that he began competing in the U.S. Chess Championship. And he won! Using some of the most incredible tactics seen in action, he became the youngest Grandmaster of chess in the United States. In fact, he would win another seven championships. And then, in 1972, he did something really incredible—he beat Boris Spassky of the Soviet Union to become the *world* champion! The chess match was held in Iceland, and it attracted more attention than any other match in history. Fischer was now the greatest chess player on the planet—and then, suddenly, he disappeared. *Poof!*

It would be nice to include Bobby Fischer in this book for only his extraordinary chess skills, but unfortunately he also had many extraordinary traits that were not so favorable. Impulsive, stubborn, obsessive, paranoid, unstable, and volatile are just a few of the adjectives that have been used to describe him. Even when he was in his prime, he made so many absurd demands that the matches almost didn't happen at all. At one point he complained about camera noises that nobody else could hear, and refused to play until the match was moved to a new location.

And even after Fischer's disappearance from society, his stubbornness led him to turn down huge opportunities, including a $1.4 million offer to defend his title. He said the money wasn't enough.

Just three years after Fischer's big win, the World Chess Federation stripped him of his championship title for failing to defend it against Anatoly Karpov. For nearly twenty years, Fischer kept a low profile, his whereabouts generally unknown. Finally, in 1992, he emerged from isolation for a rematch with Boris Spassky. Fischer won, but because the game was played in violation of international sanctions against Yugoslavia and its dictator Slobodan Milosevic, he became a wanted man by the American government.

For the remaining thirty years of Fischer's life, he more or less hid in Hungary, Yugoslavia, Argentina, the Philippines, Japan, and, ultimately, Iceland. The few public appearances he made were laced with tirades against America, Israel, and Jews (although he was born Jewish).

Bobby Fischer, one of the greatest chess players who ever lived, died at the age of sixty-four from kidney failure. He had lived one year for each square on a chessboard.

THE GOOD

First of all, you should learn the term "brilliancy." It refers to a game that is played with spectacular strategy and beauty, typically featuring unexpected moves and ingenious ideas. In other words, the game is *extraordinary*! At age thirteen, Bobby Fischer won a brilliancy against twenty-six-year-old Donald Byrne. It became known as the Game of the Century. To this day, that game is scrutinized and revered by advanced chess players around the world.

THE BAD

Fischer was incredibly paranoid—afraid that people were out to get him. He kept bottles of pills, herbal potions, and even a juicing machine stashed away so that he could feed himself if people tried to poison him. His most cherished items, which included correspondences with President Richard Nixon, were kept hidden away behind two combination locks in a secret storage room. *Yeesh.*

THE UGLY

Hours after the September 11, 2001, terrorist attacks, Bobby Fischer spoke on a radio station in the Philippines, saying, "America should be wiped out." He also wrote a letter to Osama bin Laden praising him for his achievement. Not cool, Bobby.

On a windy Saturday in 1980, near St. John's, Newfoundland—as far to the east as you can go in Canada—twenty-two-year-old Terry Fox dipped his right leg into the Atlantic Ocean and then set out to run across the country. He planned to run 26 miles (42 kilometres) a day (the distance of an entire marathon) with one artificial leg.

Just three years earlier, Fox was diagnosed with osteosarcoma, an aggressive type of bone cancer that often starts near the knee. Doctors told him that his leg would need to be amputated, and that even with chemotherapy he would have only a 50 percent chance of survival. He also learned that just a few years earlier, his survival rate would have been a mere 15 percent, but thanks to cancer research, his outlook had improved.

Inspired to make a difference, after just fourteen months of training on his artificial leg, Fox began his Marathon of Hope, an effort to raise money and awareness for cancer research. It didn't matter if it was snowing, pouring rain, or 90 degrees (32 degrees Celsius): He would run every day, seeking donations along the way.

At first, very few people knew about his mission, and not much money was raised. But after two months, he was invited to kick off a Canadian Football League game in Ontario. At the arena, the audience erupted with a standing ovation. From there, crowds continued to grow, cheering for him along his journey, and contributing money to his cause.

Fox then wanted to raise a dollar for every Canadian citizen—$24 million CAD in all. Unfortunately, on his 143rd day, as he approached the city of Thunder Bay, 3,339 miles (5,374 kilometres) from his starting point, he stopped because he was having difficulty breathing. His cancer had returned and had spread to his lungs, and he would need to undergo more treatment. A few days later, a telethon was held in his name, raising $10 million CAD to add to the $2 million CAD he had already received.

Terry Fox lost his battle with cancer on June 28, 1981, but won something much larger for all of humankind.

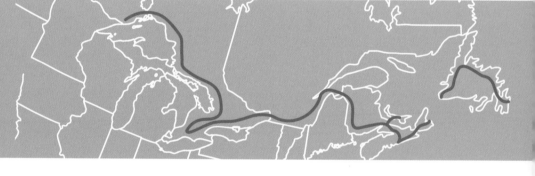

TERRY FOX'S TREK ACROSS CANADA

IN HONOR OF TERRY

- In 1982 a Canadian stamp was released with Terry Fox's image.
- In Thunder Bay, a statue depicts Terry in full stride, facing west.
- In the Canadian Rocky Mountains, there is a peak named Mount Terry Fox.
- In 1999 Terry Fox was voted Canada's Greatest Hero in a national survey.
- At the time of writing this, more than $600 million CAD has been raised for cancer research in Terry's name.

A SHORT POEM FOR TERRY

I would guess that Terry Fox
Must have gone through lots of socks.
Then again, with just one foot,
That's half the socks to go kaput.
But, fun aside, he inspired a nation,
And now we have the Terry Fox Foundation.
Although our hero is long gone.
The good he did will carry on.

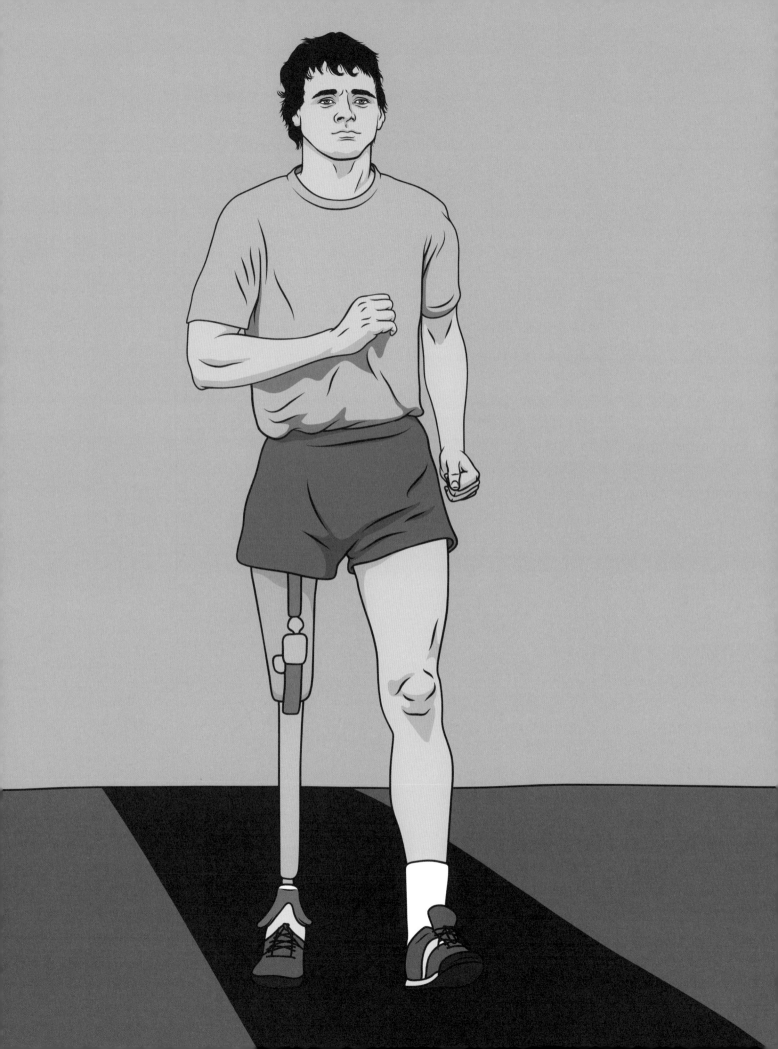

BENJAMIN FRANKLIN

Author, printer, theorist, postmaster, scientist, musician, inventor, and founding father of the United States! Yep, that can only be our pal, Ben Franklin. As a scientist, he is best known for his work in electrical theory, discovering many of the laws by which electricity operates. He also came up with some amazing inventions like bifocals, the Franklin stove, the lightning rod, and my personal favorite, the glass armonica.

As a writer, Franklin's most notable work was *Poor Richard's Almanack*, a series of reference books full of witty sayings and crafty writing, published under the alias Richard Saunders.

Later in his life, Franklin became incredibly active in politics. Perhaps his most important role was serving as a diplomat in France. Thanks to his friendship with the French government, he was able to secure their help with the Revolutionary War, which ultimately led to the United States' victory over and independence from England. To boot, Franklin was one of the five men who drafted the Declaration of Independence, which he also signed.

In case that's not enough, he also signed three other key documents in American history: the Treaty of Alliance with France, the Treaty of Peace with Great Britain, and the Constitution of the United States. And that's why Ben Franklin ruled.

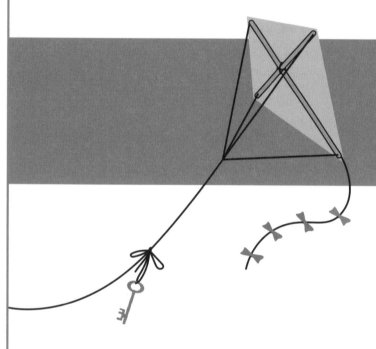

PATENT NOT PENDING

Franklin did not patent any of his inventions. He felt that they should be available to everyone, with the simple notion of making the world a better place.

ZZZZZT!!

It's true: Benjamin Franklin *did* fly a kite in a thunderstorm so that he could study the basic principles of electricity. However, it is highly unlikely that the kite was actually struck by lightning—otherwise it might have been the end of him. (Incidentally, several other scientists attempted the same experiment and were electrocuted.) Even without a lightning bolt, Franklin was able to draw a static charge from the sky, helping to prove many of his theories on electricity.

GLASS ARMONICA

But what is a glass armonica? It's a series of glass bowls attached to a spinning rod. You play this instrument by pressing your moistened fingers against the edge of the rotating bowls, creating friction—sort of like playing a wineglass (if you've ever played a wineglass). While the original glass armonica relied on a manually pumped foot pedal to keep the bowls spinning, the modern version of this instrument (yes, they still exist if you look hard enough) uses a simple electric motor. Good thing Franklin also helped figure out that whole electricity thing.

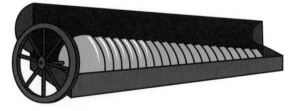

"Of all my inventions, the glass armonica has given me the greatest personal satisfaction." —Ben Franklin

BUCKMINSTER FULLER

BORN IN MILTON, MA • DIED IN LOS ANGELES, CA • 1895–1983

"Bucky," as he liked to be called (seriously), is perhaps best known for his development of the geodesic dome. He was a key innovator of the 20th century, believing in the simple principle of creating "more with less."

Fuller's intent was to develop products that could easily be manufactured and mass-produced as sustainably and efficiently as possible. The geodesic dome, for example, when applied to houses and buildings, would be cost-effective and durable, and could enclose larger amounts of space without the obstacle of support beams. He received a patent for the structure in 1954, and today there are more than 300,000 geodesic domes around the world—including housing units, military structures, and the "Spaceship Earth" ride at Epcot Center.

Some of his other designs include the three-wheeled Dymaxion car, a vehicle that could maneuver into very tight spaces; the Dymaxion house, an energy-efficient structure made for easy shipping and assembly; and the Dymaxion World Map, which shows the entire planet on a flat surface while preserving the size and shape of various land masses.

Fuller was a humanist, and believed that society would soon rely mainly on renewable sources of energy, such as solar and wind power. He predicted a time of "omni-successful education and sustenance of all humanity." Today we continue to hope that Bucky's dream becomes a reality.

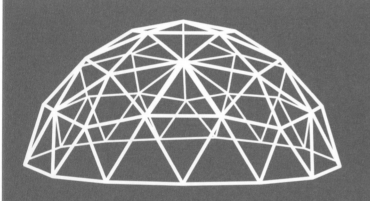

GEODESIC DOME

The geodesic dome, which approximates a sphere or semisphere by connecting multiple triangles, was widely popularized by Buckminster Fuller. The invention of the dome, however, is credited to the German engineer Walther Bauersfeld in 1922.

DYMAXION CAR

The term "Dymaxion" was a brand name created by Buckminster Fuller. It is a combination of the words "dynamic," "maximum," and "tension."

The term "innawerd" is a word that I just came up with. It is a combination of the words "innovative," "awesome," and "nerd."

VINCENZO GALILEI

BORN IN SANTA MARIA A MONTE, ITALY • DIED IN FLORENCE, ITALY • 1520–1591

Strangely enough, if you search the web for "most important people in music," you'll find a lot of references to Michael Jackson, Elvis Presley, and Kanye West. Hmm. But what about Duke Ellington and Miles Davis? Bach, Beethoven, and Brahms? Mozart and Mendelssohn? It would have been interesting to see what any of them would have done without Vincenzo Galilei, a lute player, composer, and music theorist who is credited as being the first person to advocate twelve-tone equal temperament—that is, the relative pitches on a piano as we know them today.

In large part, because of Galilei's push for equal temperament in music, as well as his development of opera, many people believe his work was a key factor in advancing us from the Renaissance era into the Baroque era. Of course, the Baroque era led to the Classical era. The Classical era led to the Romantic era. The Romantic era led to the 20th century. And the 20th century led to, um, Miley Cyrus.

WHAT EXACTLY IS TWELVE-TONE EQUAL TEMPERAMENT, YOU ASK?

If you take an entire octave on a piano, guitar, violin, or almost any instrument, and divide it into twelve equally spaced intervals, you have twelve-tone equal temperament. But why not divide it into thirteen, or sixty-seven, or some other number? Well, you can! In fact, many musicians have. However, it becomes music that most of our ears are not used to hearing—and my guess is that it wouldn't sound too good with Kanye West's music.

440 Hz   880 Hz

LIKE FATHER, LIKE SON

Vincenzo Galilei was indeed the father of the great Galileo Galilei. And Galileo Galilei, in turn, is the father of modern science and modern physics. No doubt Vincenzo influenced Galileo to research, experiment, and think for himself.

HOW DID GALILEI MAKE A LIVING?

He had a patron—a fellow named Giovanni de' Bardi, who admired Galilei so much that he provided him with money. In fact, Galilei was part of a group of musicians known as the Florentine Camerata (the Florence chamber), who would meet from time to time at Bardi's house to discuss literature, science, and the arts. Pretty cool! Somebody go find me a patron . . .

That doesn't look like a telescope—but it is!

JANE GOODALL

BORN IN LONDON, ENGLAND • 1934–

Jane Goodall is without a doubt the world's leading expert on chimpanzees. How did she get this rank? She *is* a chimpanzee! Not really, but she has spent enough time in the Gombe forest in Tanzania to witness the lives of three generations of chimps. In fact, she was the first person to discover that chimpanzees not only use tools to hunt for food, but they also *make* the tools! Prior to this finding, it was assumed that only humans made tools. Go figure?

A ton of coverage from magazines and films helped turn Goodall into a star. Today she runs the Jane Goodall Institute, devoting her time to advocacy for chimpanzees and the environment.

WHICH OF THESE QUOTES DID NOT COME FROM JANE GOODALL?

1. "My mission is to create a world where we can live in harmony with nature."
2. "I wanted to talk to the animals like Dr. Dolittle."
3. "One banana, two banana, three banana, four. Four bananas make a bunch and so do many more."

Answer: (3). It's a lyric from the theme song to the 1960s TV show *The Banana Splits Adventure Hour*. But it's highly possible that Jane Goodall has spoken those words at some point in her life.

In 1960 Goodall witnessed chimps removing leaves from twigs and then using the twigs to fish for termites from termite nests. After reporting Goodall's discovery, British archaeologist Louis Leakey famously responded, "Now we must redefine 'tool,' redefine 'man,' or accept chimpanzees as humans."

PANT-HOOT

The vocalization of a chimpanzee is known as a *pant-hoot*. Jane Goodall has spent a lot of time pant-hooting to audiences around the world.

OOH OOH AHH AHH AHHHH AHHHHH!

TEMPLE GRANDIN

BORN IN BOSTON, MA • 1947–

It has been reported that one in every eighty-eight children in the United States has some level of autism. But what is autism? Well, it's a brain condition that appears during early childhood that makes it difficult for you to communicate and interact with others. Symptoms can include repetitive behavior (such as rocking in place or saying the same words over and over again), a lack of understanding and empathizing with others, a need for sameness (such as driving the same route to school every day), and having an unusual focus on small details (such as the wheels on a toy truck instead of the whole truck). Many people with autism are extra sensitive to light and sound, and may describe a soft touch as painful or a deep touch as calming. Others may not feel pain at all.

Grandin is one such person. Diagnosed with autism early in life, her parents did everything they could to help her. They provided speech therapy, and taught her to better communicate. Although she had few friends in school and was often made fun of, she persevered. She went to college, ultimately earning a doctoral degree in animal science.

Soon after, Grandin began working as a consultant to companies with animal slaughterhouses. Her goal was to help figure out how to improve the animals' quality of life, in particular, easing the stress associated with their environment.

Because of her own autism, which included acute sensitivity to the smallest details around her, Grandin has been able to better understand how cows and other animals think. With this insight, she has helped develop methods to alleviate anxiety, not just in animals, but in people with autism throughout the world. And for that, she is extraordinary!

SQUEEZE BOX

Not to be confused with an accordion (which is also sometimes called a "squeeze box"), Temple Grandin designed a "Hug Machine" for humans, based on the containers used to hold cattle during immunization. She found that the structure was helpful in managing anxiety for herself, and ultimately for other people with autism. Today, Grandin says she no longer uses a hug machine. "It broke two years ago, and I never got around to fixing it. I'm into hugging people now."

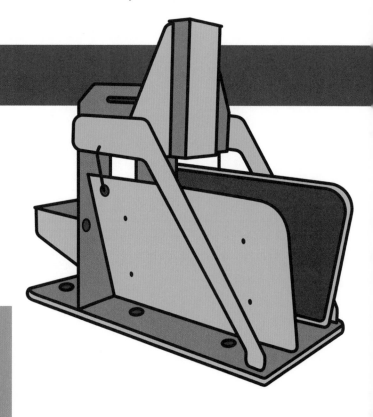

Grandin came up with the brilliant idea to corral animals through narrow and curved passages, ultimately reducing stress in animals being led to slaughter. Poor animals . . . but at least the quality of their life is much better. She said, "I think using animals for food is an ethical thing to do, but we've got to do it right. We've got to give those animals a decent life, and we've got to give them a painless death. We owe the animal respect."

HETTY GREEN

BORN IN NEW BEDFORD, MA • DIED IN NEW YORK, NY • 1834–1916

"The Witch of Wall Street"—an unfortunate nickname for a woman who had it all . . . at least in the form of money. For a time, Hetty Green was the richest woman in America, an heiress to two fortunes made from whaling in Massachusetts. Hetty reinvested her money in Civil War bonds, ultimately becoming worth nearly $200 million (equal to about $4.3 billion today).

Unfortunately, Green was mostly extraordinary because of her stinginess. She was a notorious miser. In other words, she avoided spending money at all costs (or rather, no costs). She once said, "My father taught me never to owe anyone anything, not even kindness."

And that's exactly how she lived her life. Although she was an attractive young woman, she dismissed just about every man who tried to woo her, certain that they were only after her for her money. Finally, in 1867, she married a wealthy trader from Vermont named Edward Green (whom she only partially trusted because he had his own fortune).

Hetty and Edward had two children together, Ned and Sylvia. And although she was a devoted mother, when her son became injured in a sledding accident, she took him to a charity doctor who lacked the ability to properly take care of Ned's injury. Several years later, her son's leg had to be amputated. Ick!

Green eventually decided she could no longer live with her husband, largely because she was uncomfortable with his "lavish" style of living. She began wearing a black dress that she never changed, and thus it became so tattered and filthy that it had a greenish tint. After Edward died in 1902, she began wearing a widow's veil to complete her morbid, bag-lady costume. As she walked through the streets of lower Manhattan, people were quick to recognize her. "Look, there goes the Witch of Wall Street!"

IT HAS BEEN SAID THAT HETTY GREEN WAS SO STINGY THAT . . .

. . . she never turned on the heat or used hot water.
. . . she told her laundress to wash only the hems of her dresses.
. . . she mostly ate pies that cost fifteen cents.
. . . she carried all her important documents around in suitcases and boxes instead of simply renting an office.
. . . she often carried scraps of lunch in her handbag, which she'd reheat on a radiator.

Hetty Green rarely traveled with more than a few dollar bills (though she did keep bonds worth hundreds of thousands of dollars stashed in secret pockets). At one point, a banker nervously suggested that she would be safer traveling by private carriage. She turned to the banker and said, "Perhaps you can afford to ride in a carriage—I cannot."

SKIM vs. WHOLE

While visiting a friend, Green got into an argument with a cook. She accused the cook of squandering money by using whole milk instead of skim. In mid-argument, she suffered a stroke from which she never recovered. Hetty Green died in 1916 at the age of eighty-one.

BUT WHERE DID ALL THE MONEY GO?

After Green's death, the money was passed on to her children, who were significantly less stingy. When Ned passed away in 1936, the entire estate ended up in Sylvia's hands, who in turn donated all but $1 million of the $200 million to sixty-four charities including colleges, churches, and hospitals. Good riddance!

HILDEGARD OF BINGEN

BORN IN BERMERSHEIM VOR DER HÖHE, HOLY ROMAN EMPIRE •
DIED IN BINGEN AM RHEIN, HOLY ROMAN EMPIRE 1098–1179

There are many, many extraordinary musicians and writers. But what about someone who was both, and much more—almost a thousand years ago!

If there ever was a "Jill" of all trades, it was Hildegard of Bingen. She proved herself during the Middle Ages (approximately 500 to 1500 C.E.) as a writer, philosopher, mystic, Benedictine abbess (a super nun), visionary, and the first composer whose biography is known. One of her more famous works, *Ordo Virtutum*, is perhaps the oldest surviving morality play (a popular type of play from the medieval period). It contains sixty-nine musical compositions, including several parts for voice and a speaking role for the Devil!

Although women were generally considered lesser during the Middle Ages, Hildegard was well respected by ordinary and powerful people alike. Bishops, popes, and kings often consulted her for her wisdom. Among her writings are three books of visions, which were elaborately decorated and illustrated. Her writing describes the powers of the natural world within plants, animals, and stones, as well as their healing capabilities.

One of Hildegard's most incredible feats was her invention of an alternative alphabet. It was based on a form of Latin, but contained many variations of words as well as entirely *new* words.

And that is why Hildegard of Bingen is considered one of the greatest women of her time . . . and also why she's in this book.

BEYOND THE MIDDLE

Although Hildegard lived in the middle of the Middle Ages in a region that is now part of the middle of Germany, she lived well past her middle age. In fact, she lived to be eighty-one. Pretty impressive for the Middle Ages.

ALL IN HER HEAD

It is now believed that many of Hildegard's "visions" were likely a result of severe migraine headaches.

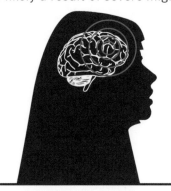

ODE TO HILDEGARD

Oh Hildegard, oh Hildegard,
For you I have utmost regard.
You were really quite the bard.
Mystics were your calling card.
Today you would be avant-garde.
Your fans would likely be die-hard.
You'd probably own a Saint Bernard.
*Of course, you'd need a bigger yard.
(That last sentence didn't need to be starred.)
Oh Hildegard, oh Hildegard.

HARRY HOUDINI

Meet Harry Houdini, the death-defying escape artist and master mystifier who astonished audiences around the world with his escapes from handcuffs, ropes, chains, straitjackets . . . often while hanging upside down or submerged in a tank of water!

As a teenager, he started performing magic tricks around New York City, first with his friend Jacob Hyman (together, they called themselves the Brothers Houdini) and later with his wife, Bess Rahner. It quickly became apparent that the escape acts were much more popular than the magic tricks, so Houdini began focusing on such grand illusions as shattering iron chains and wiggling his way out of a straitjacket, often while facing nail-biting situations such as dangling high above a sidewalk.

Houdini was also a master of promotion. He would use these public performances as a means to lure people into a larger theater (where he would charge a ticket fee), and then perform his real tricks. With extensive touring and a lot of press, Houdini became the most famous magician in the world.

While on tour in 1926, Houdini was backstage talking to a couple of college students who asked him if it was true that he was able to withstand any punch to the stomach. Yes, he said he could, if he had time to properly prepare his muscles. Unfortunately, one of the young men struck him several times before he was ready, and ruptured his appendix. Although he performed the show that night (no doubt, in a lot of pain), a few days later he was hospitalized. His appendix was removed, but it was too late—a bad infection had set in. Harry Houdini died on Halloween night in 1926 at the age of fifty-six.

To this day, people still wonder how some of Houdini's tricks worked. But as he always said, it wasn't about the tricks: It was about his hard work and imagination. And to this day, there hasn't been a magician greater than Harry Houdini.

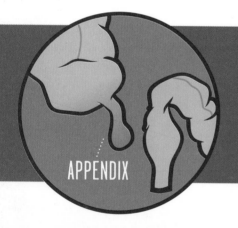

APPENDIX

BUT WAIT . . .

Was it the punches to the stomach that took down the great Houdini? There is now speculation that Houdini was already suffering from early stages of appendicitis when the incident occurred. Hmm. Well, whatever the case may be, multiple blows to the gut certainly didn't help. Youch!

NAME THAT ESCAPE ARTIST

Houdini was born Ehrich Weisz. He changed his last name to Houdini in tribute to one of his heroes, Jean Eugène Robert-Houdin, known as the father of modern magic. His first name, Harry, sounded similar to his nickname, Ehrie. Incidentally, at the time, some people thought that adding an *I* to the end of a name was a popular way to pay tribute to earlier magicians. I suppose if *you* wanted to pay tribute to Houdini, you could change your name to Houdini-i.

WHO DID IT? HOUDINI DID IT! THAT'S WHO DID IT.

Houdini did it—there he goes.
How'd he do it? No one knows.
Did he pick the locks with just his toes?
His secrets he shall not expose.

Houdini escaped again, I hear.
From under water without scuba gear!
Held his breath for three minutes . . . oh dear.
The crowds gave him a roaring cheer.

WILLIAM KAMKWAMBA

BORN IN DOWA, MALAWI • 1987–

At the age of fourteen, William Kamkwamba single-handedly built a windmill in his village in Malawi using tractor fan blades, bicycle parts, and scraps he found at a local junkyard. His makeshift windmill generated enough electricity to power four lights and two radios in his family home.

Here it should be pointed out that the Republic of Malawi is a landlocked country in southeast Africa. It is one of the least developed nations in the world, and as a result, the Malawian people are incredibly poor and lack many of the basic resources Westerners often take for granted. In fact, William's village didn't even have electricity or drinking water.

One day (soon after dropping out of school because his parents couldn't afford the tuition), William had visited the library and looked at a book called *Using Energy*. The book showed pictures of windmills, and a lightbulb suddenly lit up over his head (pun intended). Although he couldn't read English very well, by looking at the diagrams he was able to learn how to make the necessary components to harness the wind and turn it into electricity.

At first the people of his village thought he was crazy, but then they heard the radio in his home playing local Malawian reggae, and realized what William had done. Since then, he has built several more windmills, as well as a solar-powered pump that supplies fresh water.

Needless to say, the villagers of Masitala are very proud of William Kamkwamba. Thanks to him, their future is looking much brighter (pun intended).

WILLIAM'S WONDERFUL WINDMILL

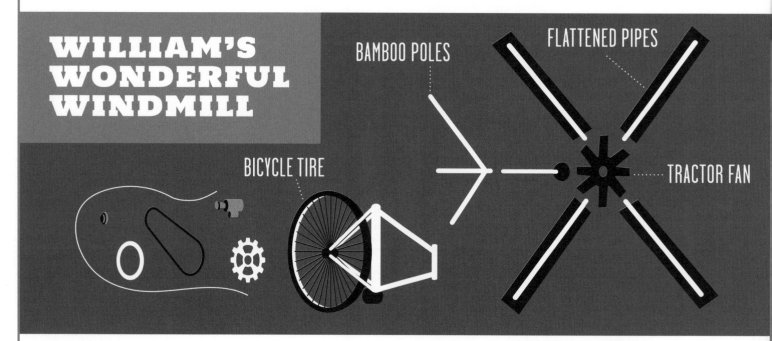

BAMBOO POLES

FLATTENED PIPES

BICYCLE TIRE

TRACTOR FAN

GOOGLE IT!

Word spread of William's incredible achievement, and in 2007 he was invited to Tanzania to appear at a conference. While there, he was asked if he needed to use the Internet, or check anything on Google. He asked, "What animal is Google?"

ONWARD AND UPWARD

William has since received scholarships allowing him to return to school. He currently studies engineering at Dartmouth University.

HELEN KELLER

BORN IN TUSCUMBIA, AL • DIED IN EASTON, CT • 1880–1968

Chances are you've heard of Helen Keller. But just in case you haven't, here goes. When she was just eighteen months old, she contracted an illness (likely scarlet fever or meningitis) that left her deaf and blind. Her childhood was extraordinarily difficult, as you can imagine. Thankfully, however, just a few days before Helen's seventh birthday, her teacher, Anne Sullivan, stepped into the scene.

Sullivan helped Helen learn how to express herself with language. She would have Helen feel objects, such as dolls and running water, and then spell out the word "d-o-l-l" or "w-a-t-e-r" in the other hand. It clicked for Helen, and soon she knew thousands of words, giving her the ability to communicate. In fact, her drive for knowledge was relentless. She learned Braille and began reading books and poetry by such greats as Oliver Wendell Holmes and Henry Wadsworth Longfellow. Helen wanted more than to simply exist in the world—she wanted to experience the world!

Keller became a student at Radcliffe College, where she wrote her autobiography, *The Story of My Life*, as well as other articles and books revealing her struggles. She quickly became famous worldwide, and was introduced to such luminaries as John D. Rockefeller, Eleanor Roosevelt, Dwight D. Eisenhower, Jawaharlal Nehru, Martha Graham, Douglas Fairbanks, John F. Kennedy, Charlie Chaplin, and Mark Twain (who would stock her bathroom with whiskey and cigars whenever she came to visit).

Keller devoted much of her time to visiting wounded soldiers, in particular those who had lost their sight. She kept immensely busy writing books, lecturing, and touring as a vaudeville act with Anne Sullivan. She even learned how to swim and ride a bicycle (though probably not at the same time). Ultimately, Helen Keller brought hope and inspiration to people with disabilities throughout the world by showing how she overcame countless obstacles.

EXTRAORDINARY HELEN KELLER QUOTES

"To be blind is to see the bright side of life."
"The highest result of education is tolerance."
"Life is either a daring adventure, or nothing."
"Keep your face to the sun and you will never see the shadows."
"Cultivate love for love is the light that gives the eye to see great and noble things."

DID YOU KNOW?

It was Alexander Graham Bell, inventor of the telephone, who helped find Helen's teacher, Anne Sullivan. Bell had also once been a teacher at a school for the deaf.

ANNE SULLIVAN

Really, Sullivan should have her own page in this book. The woman came from an orphanage, was practically blind herself, and still managed to teach Keller how to communicate and function in society, and then, as if that wasn't enough, she stayed with her for forty-nine years! Keller would say that the most important day in her whole life was the one when Sullivan came to her.

Not only did Billie Jean King win thirty-nine Grand Slam titles in tennis (ranking number one in the world for five years), but she also won several grand slams for women's rights all around the globe! She started a professional women's tennis tour, a women's sports magazine, and a women's sports foundation. But perhaps what she is best remembered for is beating the socks off of Bobby Riggs in what became known as the "Battle of the Sexes" match of 1973.

Bobby Riggs, a former Wimbledon champion and self-proclaimed "tennis hustler," contended that women's abilities were no match to men's, and that even a fifty-five-year-old man like himself could beat any current top female player. King set Riggs straight by defeating him in a televised match viewed by an estimated fifty million people worldwide. She later said, "I thought it would set us back fifty years if I didn't win that match. It would ruin the women's tour and affect all women's self-esteem."

Without a doubt, King's greater mission in life has been to assure gender equity in sports. And in numerous ways, she has done just that. A round of applause for Billie Jean King, please.

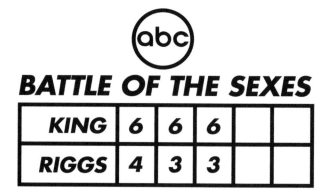

BATTLE OF THE SEXES					
KING	6	6	6		
RIGGS	4	3	3		

DID YOU KNOW?

For most of King's wins, the prize money (for her, as a woman) was just a third of the men's. She pushed for equal pay, and became the first female athlete to win more than $100,000 in a single season.

SPEAKING OF EQUALITY

Billie Jean King became one of the first prominent American athletes to publicly reveal having a gay relationship. Brava!

HOW ABOUT THAT!

- In 1975 the readers of *Seventeen* magazine voted King the most admired woman in the world. Former Israeli Prime Minister Golda Meir took second place.
- In 1990 *Life* magazine named King one of the "100 Most Important Americans of the 20th Century."
- In 2013 Michael Hearst named Billie Jean King one of the most extraordinary athletes of all time.

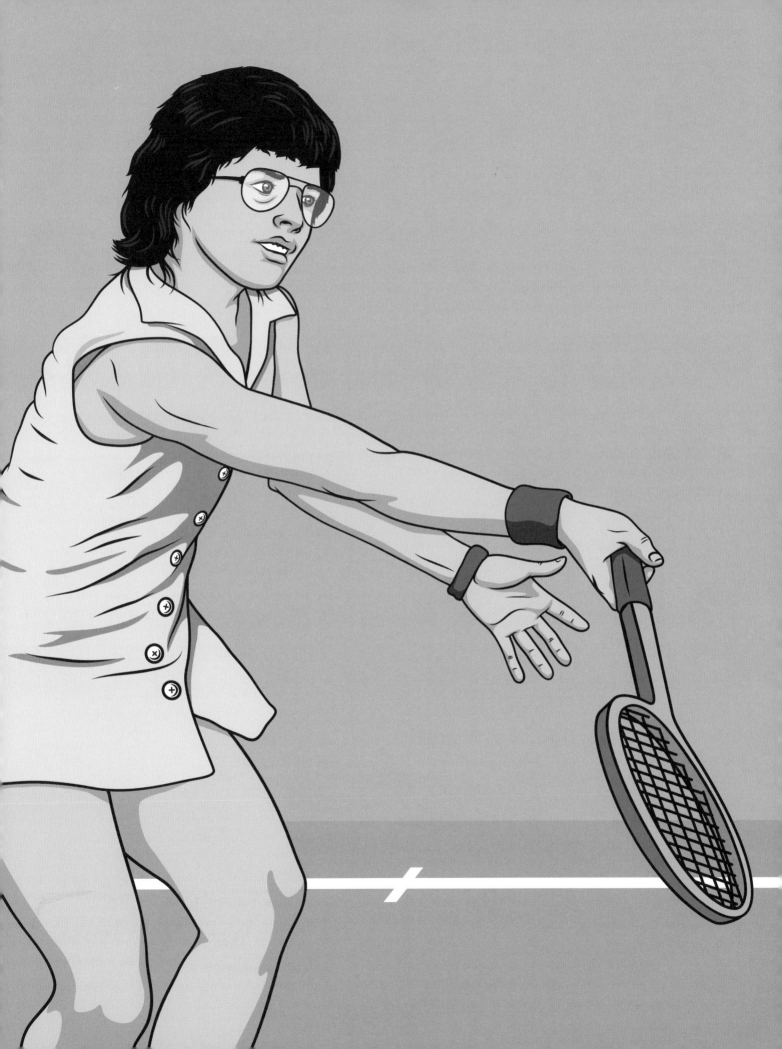

EVEL KNIEVEL

Able to jump fourteen Greyhound buses in a single bound . . . er, rather, leap of faith, Evel Knievel is perhaps the best-known American daredevil to have lived. During his fifteen-year career he attempted hundreds of jumps, flying high above water fountains, canyons, and rows of parked vehicles. And in the process he also broke at least 433 bones, received multiple concussions, and even ended up in a month-long coma after a failed jump over the fountains at Caesars Palace in Las Vegas. Nonetheless, most of his jumps were successful, and at the height of his career Knievel earned $25,000 per event. Unfortunately, he also had a temper and got into a fight, which led to a lawsuit, which led to bankruptcy. Kids, please don't try any of this at home . . . or at Caesars Palace.

AWFUL KNOFEL AND EVIL KNIEVEL

As a young man, Robert Craig Knievel was arrested—some say for stealing hubcaps, others say for reckless driving. Whatever the case might have been, he was taken to jail, where the police were also holding a man named Knofel, whom they called "Awful Knofel."

The police decided to call Robert "Evil Knievel." Robert liked his new name, and years later he legally changed it to Evel. He also switched the *I* to *E* because he thought it looked cooler.

Knievel jumping fourteen Greyhound buses in 1975.

NOTE: The record for longest motorcycle jump is not held by Evel Knievel, but rather by Robbie Maddison at 346 feet (105.5 metres)—more than twice Knievel's greatest distance.

LOOK OUT, ELVIS!

EVEL KNIEVEL IS HERE!

NOT RECOMMENDED

. . . just in case you were thinking otherwise.

SERGEI KOROLEV

On April 12, 1961, Russian cosmonaut Yuri Gagarin became the first person to travel into outer space. But the unrecognized mastermind of this amazing feat was a brilliant Soviet rocket engineer named Sergei Korolev, considered by many to be the father of practical astronautics.

From the time he was a teenager, Korolev had a strong interest in aeronautics. At seventeen he had already designed a glider, which was constructed by a Ukrainian aviation society. In 1930 Korolev began to realize the potential of liquid-fueled rocket engines and their potential use in space travel. Unfortunately, he fell out of favor with the Soviet regime, and was forced into a *gulag* (slave labor camp) for several years. Under orders from the Soviet government, he continued to work on rocketry, even while in prison.

Eventually Korolev was released, and although the Soviet military was particularly interested in rocket technology for ICBMs (intercontinental ballistic missiles), Korolev remained intent on their use for space travel. At that time, because of strong tensions and a battle for power and prestige between the Soviet Union and the United States, Korolev was commissioned to develop the first artificial satellite—*Sputnik*!

With its success, just a month later, *Sputnik 2* was sent into space under Korolev's continued management, this time carrying a dog named Laika. Korolev then turned his attention to the idea of human spaceflight. After the Soviets made several more successful (and unfortunately a few unsuccessful) missions into space over the course of ten years, with as many as fifty-seven dogs, Yuri Gagarin became the first human to journey into outer space.

Even long after Korolev's death at the age of fifty-nine (likely hastened by his years of suffering in prison), his work laid the foundation for much of modern space travel.

DID YOU KNOW?

- Although *Sputnik 1* seemingly did nothing beyond sending radio blips from its antennae, it in fact did much more: It proved that the Soviets had the capability to send a satellite into orbit. And now there are more than eight hundred manmade satellites orbiting Earth—and we have eight bazillion channels to choose from on satellite TV.
- The word "satellite" refers to anything that orbits something else. The moon is a satellite of Earth.
- It has been said that Korolev really loved many of the dogs that were sent into space. Thankfully, most of the dogs *did* survive. We hope they received Hero of Soviet Labour Awards upon their return, or at least the canine equivalent.

- Korolev thought of Yuri Gagarin as a son. When Gagarin died (not in space), a photo of Korolev was found in his wallet.
- Because of the Cold War between the Soviet Union and the United States, Korolev's achievements were not known to the world until many years after his death.

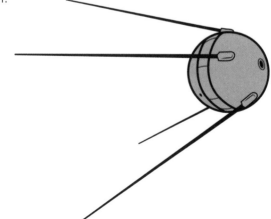

MINAKATA KUMAGUSU

BORN IN WAKAYAMA, JAPAN • DIED IN WAKAYAMA, JAPAN • 1867–1941

Some people collect rocks, some collect stamps . . . and some collect **slime mold**! Minakata Kumagusu was a true eccentric and perhaps one of the most renowned slime mold collectors of all time.

As a child, Minakata loved books. In fact, he loved them so much that he copied many by hand. While in elementary school he became particularly fascinated by an encyclopedia, and took it upon himself to copy the entire set!

School itself, however, was not so interesting to him. After attending Tokyo University for a short time, he dropped out to travel to the United States. With very little money, he set out on a journey to do what he loved most—collect and research slime mold. From California to Michigan to Florida he traveled, writing about the various fungi and plants he encountered along the way. Other stops included Cuba and the West Indies, where for a brief period he traveled with a circus, working as an elephant driver's assistant.

Minakata ended up in London where he worked at the British Museum, continuing his research on slime mold at a higher level. He was offered a job at the museum, but declined. Eventually he returned to Japan in rags, but with *lots* of specimens and *lots* of notes. Back in his native country he was honored to meet the young Emperor Hirohito, a keen biologist. Minakata presented him with a gift of 110 rare specimens. Sweet!

Eventually Minakata settled down, married, and had a family. In his later years, when he was too weak to hunt for slime molds in the forest on his own, he would ask his children to collect specimens for him. His daughter would then view the fungi through a microscope and make sketches on his behalf. With his never-ending passion for slime molds, Minakata Kumagusu collected more than fourteen thousand specimens, making him a leading scholar on the subject, and marking his place as an extraordinary genius.

WHAT THE HECK *IS* SLIME MOLD, ANYWAY?

Slime molds are an organism like a plant or a mushroom, but they can do something that mushrooms can't do—they can crawl for their food! Very, very slowly. You can typically find them on the ground in forests, often under rotting logs and piles of leaves. Although the name "slime mold" sounds incredibly disgusting, they can sometimes be quite beautiful. Go ahead, watch a slime mold video on YouTube. Kind of disgustingly awesome, I'd say.

FUNGUS AMONGUS

- Minakata Kumagusu's first published book was titled *Collection of Fungi in Michigan*. (Probably not a bestseller.)
- Minakata Kumagusu discovered a new type of slime mold on a persimmon tree in his backyard. Today, biologists around the world refer to this particular fungus as *Minakatella longifolia G. Lister.*
- He believed that there are no boundaries in research, and that all living creatures are connected in a ring of life.
- There is a Minakata Kumagusu museum in his home-town of Wakayama, Japan.

SAVE THE SHRINES!

During the early 20th century, when the Japanese government sought to tear down local shrines around the country, Minakata fought back, stating that the shrines were a symbol for Japanese nature worship. At one point he barged into a political meeting and threw chairs around the room in protest.

P.S. Are you fascinated by slime molds? Maybe you should join the Slime Mould Collective (a.k.a. SLIMOCO), "an international network of/for intelligent organisms."

68

BRUCE LEE

Don't mess with Bruce! Many people did—and many paid the price. Not just on film, but also in real life.

Bruce Lee grew up in Hong Kong during a rather turbulent time. The streets were crowded with Chinese refugees, and gang fights were a common occurrence. After Bruce faced a number of nasty fights, Bruce's father decided to train his son in martial arts. By the time Bruce was eighteen, the street fights had become so frequent and so dangerous that his parents decided to send him to America for a better and safer life.

In Seattle, while continuing his education, Lee began teaching martial arts in a style he referred to as Jun Fan Gung Fu (which translates to "Bruce Lee's Kung Fu"). He also entered several martial arts competitions in California, where he was ultimately "discovered" by Hollywood. He appeared in a season of the TV series *The Green Hornet*, and then went on to choreograph fight scenes for such movies as *The Wrecking Crew* and *A Walk in the Spring Rain*. Soon he landed leading roles in *The Big Boss* and *Fist of Fury*, which turned him into an international superstar.

Lee went on to make several more successful films until his premature death at the age of thirty-two from an apparent allergic reaction to muscle relaxers.

Throughout his short career, not only was Bruce Lee able to help change the way Asians were portrayed in film, but he also brought martial arts to the West in a way they had never been appreciated before.

DID YOU KNOW?

Bruce Lee's father, Lee Hoi-Chuen, was a famous Cantonese opera singer. He and his wife, Grace Ho, were on tour in America when Bruce was born in San Francisco's Chinatown. Bruce Lee's birth name was Lee Jun-fan, meaning "return again." His mother hoped her son would return to America when he came of age. And he did!

P.S. The name "Bruce" was likely given to Lee by the doctor who delivered him at the hospital in San Francisco.

DUDE WAS FAST!

Bruce Lee's striking speed from 3 feet (0.9 metre) away was five-hundredths of a second! His hand movements were so fast, legend has it that during filming, the camera speed had to be increased in order to see them on the screen.

5/100ths
95/100ths

A FEW MORE FUN FACTS . . .

- Bruce Lee did push-ups using just two fingers.
- Bruce Lee was an accomplished dancer and cha-cha champion.
- Bruce Lee was born during the hour and the year of the Dragon. This meant that he was pretty much destined to be awesome.

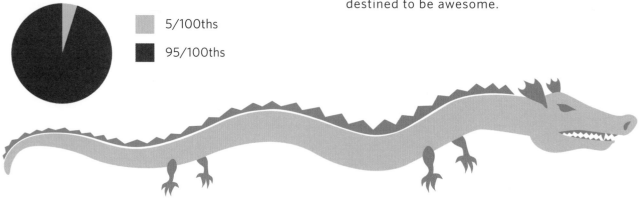

EDWARD LEEDSKALNIN

BORN IN STĀMERIENA PARISH, LATVIA • DIED IN MIAMI, FL • 1887–1951

"YOU WILL BE SEEING UNUSUAL ACCOMPLISHMENT" reads the stone-carved sign as you enter Coral Castle in Homestead, Florida. And it's true! Ed Leedskalnin, who stood just over 5 feet (1.5 metres) and weighed a mere 100 pounds (45.4 kilograms), single-handedly built a fantasy world from carved blocks of limestone. He dug the stone from the ground; shaped the massive blocks (which weighed as much as 5 to 10 tons [4.5 to 9.1 tonnes] each) into walls, furniture, fountains, sundials, and even a barbecue (!); and strategically placed them throughout the grounds.

The precision of his craftsmanship is amazingly accurate and astonishing—the front gate, an 8-foot- (2.4-metre-) tall, 8-ton (7.3-tonne) block of stone, was balanced so precisely that it could be pushed open with a single finger. The gate lasted for decades until the 1980s, at which point it was removed by six men and a 45-ton (40.8-tonne) crane. Since no one ever witnessed Leedskalnin building his stone monument, some say he had supernatural powers. Leedskalnin, on the other hand, would say that he simply knew the secrets used to build the ancient pyramids.

When Leedskalnin was asked why he built the castle, he would answer that it was for his "sweet sixteen." It is believed he was referring to Agnes Scuffs, his fiancée, who jilted him a day before their wedding in Latvia. In the 1980s, rock star Billy Idol wrote a song titled "Sweet Sixteen" and filmed the video at Coral Castle.

A BRIEF POEM FOR ED

Massive rocks are everywhere—
Precisely balanced to a hair.
A castle in the Florida sun,
A castle built for only one.
Or maybe two, his sweet sixteen?
But that was likely just a dream.
Either way, it's quite a feat:
Ed, your construct can't be beat.
It will go down in history—
The process still a mystery.
Is it physics or magic, Ed?
His secret shall remain unsaid.

STAGECOACH MARY

BORN IN HICKMAN COUNTY, TN • DIED IN CASCADE, MT • 1832-1914

Basically, Stagecoach Mary ruled! Six-foot- (1.8-metre-) tall, 200-pound (90.7-kilogram) Mary Fields smoked cigars, packed a pistol, kept a jug of whiskey at her side, and made certain the mail got delivered. She was the first African American woman to be employed as a mail carrier in the United States, and only the second woman to work for the United States Postal Service—a job she took on at the age of sixty.

Fields was born a slave and grew up as an orphan. After emancipation, she was taken under the wing of an Ohio nun named Mother Amadeus. When Mother Amadeus suddenly got sick, Fields nursed her back to health. She also took it upon herself to protect all the nuns in the convent—with a gun strapped under her apron.

Of course, this sort of toughness, while it may have been appreciated, doesn't necessarily fit in a nunnery.

Fields was ultimately dismissed from her duties. The nuns felt bad, so they provided her with enough money to start her own business.

Mary opened a café, but because she was so kind and generous, she gave food to everyone who stepped in the door (whether or not they had money) and her business was run into the ground several times.

Eventually, she closed down the café and began working a mail delivery job. She and her mule, Moses, never missed a day of work. Even if it was snowing and the wagon was frozen in its tracks, Mary would make the deliveries on foot, carrying the sacks of mail on her shoulders.

Cascade loved Stagecoach Mary. Each year on her birthday, the town would close its schools to celebrate. I say we continue that tradition!

NO WOMEN ALLOWED (EXCEPT FOR MARY FIELDS)

Although women were forbidden to enter saloons in Montana, the mayor of Cascade gave Mary Fields an exception.

GARY COOPER

The actor Gary Cooper, also a Montanan, wrote an article for *Ebony* magazine in which he said, "Born a slave somewhere in Tennessee . . . Mary lived to become one of the freest souls ever to draw a breath or a .38."

SIR, ALFRED MEHRAN

Ever missed a flight and been stuck in the airport? An hour can feel like an eternity. Can you imagine being stuck in an airport for *seventeen years*!?

In 1977 Mehran Karimi Nasseri was traveling to the United Kingdom to start a new life after being expelled from Iran for opposing political views. En route, his briefcase went missing along with all the paperwork he needed to enter Britain. He boarded the plane to London, but was returned to Paris, and from there he would eventually be sent back to Iran. However, because Iran would no longer accept him, Nasseri was stuck in limbo.

The French courts ruled that since he had entered the country legally, he could not be expelled from the airport, but they also could not grant him permission to enter France. With nowhere else to go, Nasseri made himself comfortable in Terminal 1 at Paris's Charles de Gaulle Airport.

Over the course of seventeen years at the airport, Nasseri read books—a lot of books! He also studied economics, and wrote in his diary every single day. The employees at the airport took a liking to Nasseri and supplied him with food, newspapers, and more books. "He's like a part of the airport. Everyone knows him," said the manager of the Bye Bye Bar in a 1997 *Boston Globe* interview. "That's his table, his chair, his place." A Lufthansa clerk added, "He's one of us. We even get letters from him."

Nasseri's stay at the airport finally came to an end in 2006 when he became ill and needed medical attention. After being released from a Paris hospital, with the help of the Red Cross, he was placed in a shelter, where he still lives today. He took the name "Sir, Alfred Mehran" (including the misplaced comma) from a letter given to him by British immigration.

TRUE OR FALSE?

1. The 2004 film *The Terminal*, starring Tom Hanks, is loosely based on Sir, Alfred Mehran.

2. In 1995 Belgium offered him residence; however, Mehran refused, saying that he wanted to enter the United Kingdom as he had initially intended.

3. Sir, Alfred Mehran read every single airport novel written between 1977 and 2006.

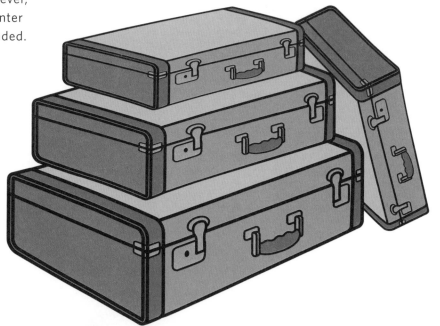

Answers: 1. T; 2. T; 3. F (then again, I wouldn't doubt it).

76

KEVIN MITNICK

BORN IN LOS ANGELES, CA • 1963-

Kevin Mitnick was once the world's most wanted hacker. He broke into countless computer systems, including those of Motorola, Sun Microsystems, Pacific Bell, and Nokia. Eventually he got caught, and spent five years in prison. In fact, during that time Mitnick was sentenced to eight months in solitary confinement so that he wouldn't have access to any technology, including a prison telephone! Why? According to Mitnick, the judge had been led to believe that Mitnick had the capability to pick up the telephone and launch a nuclear weapon by simply whistling the launch code.

Mitnick grew up in suburban Los Angeles in the 1970s, just as the computer industry began to take off. He started hacking when he was in high school, mostly because he was fascinated with the telephone system. A prankster at heart, Mitnick would change his friends' phones to pay phone status, so that when they tried to dial a number, a recorded voice would ask them to deposit a dime. A nifty trick indeed; however, one thing led to another, and eventually Mitnick was hacking into huge corporate systems—a major felony. Still, he was able to dodge the FBI for almost three years!

With his hacking skills, Mitnick would tap into phone systems and monitor the FBI agents' numbers, keeping track of their whereabouts. As the agents closed in on his location and got closer to him, he would simply move farther away. Eventually the FBI wised up to his tricks and tracked his cellular phone signal using radio gear. Kevin Mitnick was arrested on Valentine's Day in 1995; they found him in an apartment in Raleigh, North Carolina, sitting at a computer. Imagine that!

SO, WHAT'S HE DOING NOW?

Today Kevin Mitnick is an author, public speaker, and security consultant. He still hacks into systems, but now he does it to fix them before "the bad guys" get there. In fact, the same companies that once wanted to put him in prison are now hiring him to test their security.

MCHACKED

As a teenager, Kevin would hack into McDonald's drive-through systems. When customers pulled up to the intercom to place an order, they'd end up talking to Mitnick, who would be across the street speaking into a ham radio. If cops drove up, Kevin would tell them that McDonald's no longer sold burgers, only doughnuts.

THIS ENTRY ALSO EARNS THE OFFICIAL STAMP OF . . .

ILLEGALLY HACKING INTO OTHER PEOPLE'S COMPUTERS IS, WELL . . . ILLEGAL.
DON'T DO IT!

RODNEY MULLEN

BORN IN GAINESVILLE, FL • 1966–

On just about any given day, you are likely to pass kids on the street attempting to flip skateboards under their feet. Sometimes they land the tricks. Sometimes they don't. Back in the 1980s, Rodney Mullen almost always landed the tricks. After all, he invented just about all of them! And for that reason, he is often considered the "godfather of street skating."

But it wasn't an easy journey for Mullen. He grew up a loner in Gainesville, Florida. His strict father did not like the idea of skateboarding, and made a deal with his ten-year-old son that he would only be allowed to skate if he wore *all* his pads, and with the condition that the first time he became seriously injured, he would quit.

Gainesville can reach temperatures in the upper 90s (35 to 37 degrees Celsius), so in order to stay cool, and because he liked the solitude, Mullen skated mostly at night in his garage. While skaters in California were getting "radical" with their friends, learning how to "ride vert" and "catch air" on ramps and in drained-out swimming pools, he was honing his skills on flat ground, mastering the nerdier genre of skateboarding known at the time as "freestyle."

Alone at night, Mullen would flip his board upside down, backward and forward, and over and under his feet, inventing and perfecting tricks that no one had ever dreamt of before. His father finally let him enter a few contests, and he very quickly became a top competitor, winning thirty amateur freestyle contests in a row.

At the age of fourteen, Mullen turned pro, joining Powell Peralta's renowned Bones Brigade team. In the 1980s, he won thirty-four out of thirty-five competitions, often frustrating fellow competitors (and sometimes even the judges) with his amazing precision and brilliant tricks.

Rodney Mullen became the top freestyle skater of all time. Along the ride, however, he had become less and less enchanted by competition, and more interested in the sport as a means of expression. As the '80s turned to the '90s and freestyle slowly turned into the hipper genre of "street skating," he reinvented himself, applying his arsenal of flat-ground maneuvers to city curbs, embankments, benches, handrails, and every other obstacle a skater loves to encounter. In no time, he transformed into one of the greatest street skaters the world had yet to see. In addition, he also founded several companies to improve skate equipment and cultivate teams of talented riders, all with the underlying notion of simply making skateboarding better for everyone.

To this day, Mullen still loves to skate . . . but only at night when nobody is watching.

THE FLATGROUND OLLIE

The flatground ollie, invented by Rodney Mullen, is perhaps the most important trick used by street skaters today. It allows you to "leap" up onto curbs, or even flip the board under your feet. The maneuver is performed when the skater quickly pops the tail of the board against the ground and then jumps into the air, "scooping" the board up with their feet. Although a version of the trick was pioneered by Alan "Ollie" Gelfand as an aerial maneuver in swimming pools, it was Rodney Mullen who invented and developed it on flat ground.

SPORT + ART = COMMUNITY

Certainly it's a sport. But Mullen is here to remind you that what's great about skateboarding is that it can also be used as a form of expression. After more than three decades of professional skating, he and his peers have helped to carve out something much larger than what the term "sport" describes. In his own words: "All of us express ourselves through what we do, so that together we forge the distinctiveness of skateboarding as a whole."

A FEW OF THE TRICKS RODNEY MULLEN INVENTED

Flatground ollie, ollie impossible, ollie nosebones, ollie fingerflip, ollie airwalk, one-footed ollie, 540 shove-it, no-handed 50/50, 50/50 saran wrap, 50/50 casper, 360 flip, switch 360 flip, 360 pressure flip, casper 360 flip, casper slide, helipop, heelflip, kickflip, gazelle flip, ollie impossible, sidewinder, half-cab kickflip, backside 180 kickflip, frontside heelflip shove-it, kickflip underflip, darkslide, primo slide, plus countless variations of just about all of the above.

ÖTZI THE ICEMAN • 3300 B.C.E.

The Iceman is perhaps more important for what he did *after* he died than for what he did during his life. That is to say, he remained frozen and well preserved for 5,300 years! Because of this, the Iceman is one of the most important archaeological finds of all time, providing us with an incredible peek at our ancestors in Europe during the Copper Age.

The Iceman was discovered in 1991 by two German backpackers. At first they thought the body was of a recently deceased hiker, but police and, later, scientists realized just what the backpackers had actually stumbled upon. Word got out, and the local people nicknamed the frozen corpse Ötzi, after the Ötztal Valley where he was discovered.

Alongside Ötzi were several tools, including a bow, arrows, a knife, and a copper ax, which all helped archaeologists identify him as being 5,300 years old—the oldest complete mummy found to date!

How he died is still unknown. At first it was assumed that while he was attempting to cross the mountains, a nasty storm blew through, freezing him in his sleep. However, in 2001 researchers discovered that Ötzi had an arrowhead lodged in his shoulder. Further investigation showed evidence of head trauma, perhaps an attack by another tribesman. One way or another, a blanket of snow quickly covered his body after his death, freezing him perfectly for us to unearth thousands of years later. And that's truly extraordinary!

A FEW OF THE ITEMS FOUND WITH ÖTZI

- Ax with a 4-inch (10-centimetre) blade made from almost pure copper.
- A 6-foot- (1.8-metre-) long unstrung bow, and a deerskin quiver full of unfinished arrows.
- Mushrooms threaded on a leather string, and a slice of antelope meat.
- A small knife with a flint blade in a plaited grass sheath.
- A stone disk on a leather string.
- Size 6 (UK 5.5) shoes, made of bearskin and deer hide and filled with hay for warmth.
- An iPhone with a buffalo hide carrying case (just kidding).

MULTIPLE CHOICE

1. Thanks to science, we have been able to determine that Ötzi . . .
   a) died when he was around forty-five years old.
   b) suffered from Lyme disease.
   c) was allergic to milk.
   d) all of the above.
2. The Iceman stood approximately . . .
   a) 8 feet 4 inches (2.5 metres) tall.
   b) 5 feet 3 inches (1.6 metres) tall.
   c) 3 feet 6 inches (1 metre) tall.
   d) 0.06 millimeter tall (he was microscopic).
3. It is clear from Ötzi's outfit that he had been part of the touring company . . .
   a) Mountain Men on Ice.
   b) Copper Crafters on Ice.
   c) Icemen on Ice.
   d) None of the above.

CHOSEN TO BE FROZEN?

Don't think so. An arrowhead in his shoulder and wounds to the head show that Ötzi was likely attacked by another tribesman.

Answers: 1. (d); 2. (b); 3. (d).

Thanks to the discovery of Ötzi, we now have a better sense of how people dressed, the tools they used, and what they ate during the Copper Age.

SAM PATCH

BORN IN PAWTUCKET, RI • DIED IN ROCHESTER, NY • c.1799–1829

Sam Patch, a.k.a. "The Yankee Leaper," made his mark as the first well-known American daredevil. He jumped his way into fame from the top of mastheads and waterfalls throughout New York and New Jersey, performing to crowds of thousands.

Patch's first acclaimed jump took place at Passaic Falls in New Jersey on opening day for a brand new bridge that spanned the falls. It was built by a wealthy sawmill owner named Timothy Crane, who restricted access to all but those who could afford the toll.

Patch was outraged. Moments before the bridge was to open, he snuck out onto the rocks next to the falls, and shouted to the crowd that Timothy Crane has done great things, but Sam Patch would do great things as well! He then jumped feet first into the water 77 feet (23.5 metres) below, resurfacing just in time to hear the cheers from the crowd.

Nine months later, when Crane scheduled a July 4th fireworks display at the bridge to regain attention, Patch returned, making another spectacular leap. This time the newspapers printed Patch's words: "Some things can be done as well as others."

Sam Patch was now famous. He received an invitation from the city of Niagara Falls to help publicize the opening of a newly discovered cave within the falls. Patch agreed to make the jump, and a 125-foot (38.1-metre) ladder was erected at the edge of the Niagara River.

Unfortunately, Patch didn't show up—he had been on a drinking binge and missed the entire event! After a public apology, he returned two weeks later and successfully made the jump not once, but twice.

Now, Patch turned to Genesee Falls in Rochester, New York. The posters for the event stated "Higher Yet!" and "There's No Mistake in Sam Patch" and that it would be "Sam's Last Jump!" Unfortunately, that third statement was true. Well, sort of.

Patch jumped the High Falls, but it yielded so little money that he decided to schedule a second jump a week later, on Friday the 13th. To add to the excitement, he raised the height to 125 feet (38.1 metres) by building a 25-foot (7.6-metre) platform. Reports from the crowd vary: Some say he staggered while climbing the platform. Others say he unintentionally fell. Either way, he hit the water off-center, and did not return to the surface.

Many thought that Patch had secretly survived and had hidden at the base of the falls with a bottle of brandy. One newspaper went so far as to report that the entire event had been a hoax, and that it had been "a man of straw, paint, sand, and stones having substituted for the jumping hero." Alas, Sam Patch's frozen body was found the following March in the icy waters at the mouth of the Genesee River. And that's why you should never drink and dive!

A FEW FACTOIDS, JUST FOR YOU

- President Andrew Jackson named his favorite horse Sam Patch after the Yankee Leaper.
- Sam Patch's fee for jumping Niagara Falls was $75.
- Eight thousand people showed up to witness the jump at Genesee Falls. Census records for the town of Rochester the following year list the population at 9,207.
- "Some things can be done as well as others!"*

*Wait, what does that even mean?

ODE TO SAMUEL PATCH

Sam Patch, Sam Patch, the jumping bug
    he did catch.
A hundred feet without a scratch.
So impressive, Samuel Patch.

Sam Patch, Sam Patch, the fame and glory
    would soon hatch.
Plus a few bucks he would snatch.
Exciting times for Samuel Patch.

Sam Patch, Sam Patch, at Genesee Falls
    he met his match.
From his "spirits" he did detach.
So long to you, dear Samuel Patch.

GEORGE PLIMPTON

BORN IN NEW YORK, NY • DIED IN NEW YORK, NY • 1927–2003

Meet the real Curious George! Although George Plimpton wasn't actually a monkey, he *was* lanky with unbounded energy—and he definitely was curious.

As a "participatory journalist," Plimpton felt that it was important to immerse himself in whatever subject he happened to be writing about. He played ice hockey with the Boston Bruins, football with the Detroit Lions, baseball with the New York Yankees, and tennis against Pancho Gonzales; boxed against Archie Moore; and golfed against Arnold Palmer. He served as triangle player with the New York Philharmonic under Leonard Bernstein, and swung on the flying trapeze with the Clyde Beatty–Cole Brothers Circus. For a time, he also held the title of fireworks commissioner for New York City (he was a huge fan of fireworks).

In essence, Plimpton knew everybody, and did everything he could for the sake of a story. Undoubtedly, he also enjoyed the mere act of living his life to its fullest and the attention that came with it. He told his adventures in nearly three dozen books, and if that's not enough to validate his true underlying passion as a writer, he also ran *The Paris Review* literary journal for fifty years!

Oh, did I mention Plimpton also had acting roles in at least twenty films, including *Lawrence of Arabia*, *The Bonfire of the Vanities*, *Nixon*, and *Good Will Hunting*? Perhaps it would be easier to list the things that George Plimpton *didn't* do!

WHICH ONE IS NOT TRUE?

1. George Plimpton was an accomplished bird-watcher.

2. George Plimpton once rode on the back of Evel Knievel's motorcycle as he jumped the Grand Canyon.

3. George Plimpton was a close friend of Robert Kennedy's, and was with him at the Ambassador Hotel in Los Angeles when he was assassinated. Immediately after the shooting, Plimpton helped tackle shooter Sirhan Sirhan to the ground.

4. George Plimpton once arranged for world record grape catcher Paul Tavilla to catch a grape in his mouth, tossed from the top of Trump Tower.

5. A cartoon in *The New Yorker* once showed a man about to be operated on. Looking up, he asks the surgeon, "Wait a minute! How do I know you're not George Plimpton?"

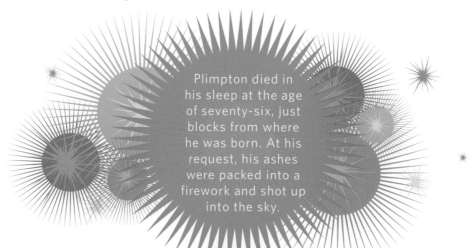

Plimpton died in his sleep at the age of seventy-six, just blocks from where he was born. At his request, his ashes were packed into a firework and shot up into the sky.

Answer: Number 2 is not true. But then again, I wouldn't put it past him.

86

ALAIN ROBERT

BORN IN DIGOIN, FRANCE • 1962–

How do you say Spider-Man in French? Well, if you look up the words "Spiderman in French," on the Internet, the first thing that appears is the name Alain Robert. What Alain does, however, might actually be more daring than Spider-Man's exploits . . . at least as far as his technique for climbing buildings is concerned. He doesn't use webs or sticky spider claws; he simply "freescales," using his bare hands with no ropes for protection, no nets below—if you fall, you die!

In fact, Robert has scaled just about all of the tallest and most notable buildings around the world. As you might guess, this is illegal in most places, and thus he has been arrested and fined numerous times. But that hasn't stopped him in the slightest, it just makes it all the more exciting!

To name a few structures Alain has conquered: the Sydney Tower in Australia (1,014 feet [309 metres]), the Eiffel Tower in Paris (1,063 feet [324 metres]), the Empire State Building in New York City (1,250 feet [381 metres]), and Taipei 101 in Taiwan (1,667 feet [508 metres]).

Robert always loved to climb, his motivations largely from the risk itself. When he was just eleven years old, after forgetting his keys, he scaled eight floors so that he could sneak back into his apartment through a window. As a teenager he began climbing the cliffs near his hometown in southern France. From there he began traveling the planet, tackling one building after another: from Cuba to China, and New York to Australia.

To this day, Alain has made more than sixty-five major climbs, and in doing so has been arrested at least a dozen times. How do you say "police record" in France? Well, if you really want to know, it's "casier judiciaire."

RAISING FUNDS, ONE FLOOR AT A TIME

In 1997 Robert climbed (without authorization) the 1,483-foot (452-metre) Petronas Towers in Kuala Lumpur, Malaysia. He was arrested and fined the equivalent of $600. The impact on the media, however, was so massive that the Sabah Foundation asked him to climb their building in Malaysia to raise funds for charity. The event drew a crowd of 15,000 and raised $150,000.

This entry earns the official stamp of

. . . on any structure more than 2 feet (0.61 metre) tall!

In 2011 Robert scaled the Burj Khalifa building in Dubai (2,717 feet [828 metres]), the world's tallest building! (For this particular climb he used some safety equipment.) The ascent took him six hours.

QUIZZZZZZ

1. The art of climbing the outside of buildings and other artificial structures is referred to as . . .
   a) urban climbing.
   b) buildering.
   c) structuring.
   d) insanity.
2. Over the course of his career, Alain Robert . . .
   a) has never fallen.
   b) only fell once, but landed on his feet, so it was *totally* okay.
   c) has fallen several times and sustained multiple severe injuries.
   d) all of the above.

Answers:
1. (a), (b), and (c) are *all* correct. Though you may as well throw in (d), too.

2. (c) is correct. Twice, he has fallen from heights of just 49 feet (15 metres), and as a result received numerous broken bones, head injuries, nerve damage, and to this day suffers from severe vertigo (dizziness) . . . but still climbs. P.S. Answer (d) makes absolutely no sense, fool.

FRED ROGERS

It was always a beautiful day in *Mister Rogers' Neighborhood*. The front door to his house would open and Mister Rogers would enter, softly singing, while changing from his coat and fancy shoes into more comfortable sneakers and a cardigan.

In a television career that spanned six decades, Fred Rogers educated millions of children on such topics as making friends, going to the doctor, and simply *being yourself*. Each episode typically included a field trip to a place such as a bakery or music shop. And at some point, there would be a trolley ride into the Neighborhood of Make-Believe, a miniature town with puppet friends who would further explore the episode's theme.

The truth is that Rogers hated television. He was determined to find a way to use it as a tool for education and nurturing. And with nerdy but sincere kindness, that's just what he did. The series first aired on CBC (Canadian Broadcasting Corporation) in Canada in 1963—just a year after Rogers was ordained as a Presbyterian minister—and then relocated to PBS in 1966. In all, *Mister Rogers' Neighborhood* contained 895 episodes, the final episode broadcasting in August 2001.

Rogers earned four daytime Emmys, an Emmy Lifetime Achievement Award, a Peabody Award, and a Presidential Medal of Freedom. Oh, yeah, and today one of his red sweaters hangs in the Smithsonian. And it is likely that if you ask just about any person in the United States or Canada born between 1940 and 1990 to finish the phrase, "Would you be mine? Could you be mine?" they will sing you the answer: "Won't you be my neighbor?"

KOKO ♥ MISTER ROGERS

Koko the gorilla, who had been taught to communicate in American Sign Language and understood many English words, loved to watch *Mister Rogers' Neighborhood*. Rogers heard about this, and decided to visit Koko for his show. Upon arrival, not only did Koko emphatically hug him, but she also began to remove his shoes.

GOOSE BUMP THE GOVERNMENT

PBS (Public Broadcasting Service) is largely funded by the government, which proposed large cuts to the TV network in 1969. Fred Rogers traveled to Washington, D.C., and appeared before a United States Senate sub-committee. He passionately argued for the importance of PBS, in particular its role in educating young people to become happy and healthy citizens. The committee chairman, John Pastore (who somehow had not heard of the show), was so moved by the speech that he later admitted it gave him goose bumps. As a result, in 1971, funding for PBS increased from $9 million to $22 million.

LEGEND HAS IT . . .

Dear Mister Rogers,

Fred Rogers's car was once stolen from a street near the TV station. He filed a police report, and the news went out over the radio about Mister Rogers's missing Chevy Impala. Two days later, the car was found in the exact same spot with a note from the thieves: "If we'd known it was yours, we never would have taken it."

DEION SANDERS

BORN IN FORT MYERS, FL • 1967–

I know what you're thinking: Deion "Prime Time" Sanders? Extraordinary? But seriously, the dude played for the NFL and the MLB—at the same time! In fact, he is the only person to have hit a Major League Baseball home run and scored a National Football League touchdown in the same week! That was in September 1989, while Sanders played simultaneously for the Atlanta Falcons and the New York Yankees. Pretty extraordinary, if you ask me.

Of course, Sanders's success came with a *touch* of ego. In fact, there are few sports stars who have exuded quite as much attitude. During his college years he began using the nickname "Prime Time" to help sell his fame, and wore gold chains and giant rings while driving around in a Chrysler convertible.

One time, after having played in a football game with the Miami Falcons, Sanders hopped on a private jet so he could play baseball with the Atlanta Braves just a few hours later. At the Braves' game, commentator Tim McCarver said on national TV that he considered Sanders's actions to be "self-centered."

Sanders took great offense at this, and a few days later (after the Braves had won the National League Championship, and McCarver was in the locker room interviewing players), Sanders dumped a bucket of ice water onto McCarver's head . . . three times, saying that McCarver "needed to cool off."

In another incident during a Yankees game, Sanders stepped up to the plate, and before the first pitch was thrown, he drew a dollar sign in the batter's box. White Sox catcher Carlton Fisk was so annoyed by Sanders' pompous behavior that he stood up and shouted at him, "There is a right way and a wrong way to play this game. You're playing it the wrong way. And the rest of us don't like it. Someday, you're going to get this game shoved right down your throat."

Regardless, Sanders's athletic ability is undeniable. In all, he played fourteen seasons in the NFL and nine with Major League Baseball. In 2011 Sanders was inducted into the Pro Football Hall of Fame. Today he spends much of his time with his organization TRUTH Sports, which aims to get kids playing sports and off the street.

In the words of Prime Time himself, "If you look good, you feel good. And if you feel good, you play good. If you play good, they pay good. And if they pay good, you eat good." Well, alrighty then.

BY THE WAY

- Sanders is the only person to have played in a Super Bowl and a World Series. While he did not win the World Series (1992, Atlanta Braves), he did win two Super Bowls (1995, San Francisco 49ers; 1996, Dallas Cowboys).
- Sanders could run the 40-yard (36.5-metre) dash in 4.27 seconds. That's fast!
- Sanders named his first son Deion Jr. and his first daughter Deiondra.
- Sanders, along with his second wife and five children, starred in a reality show called *Deion & Pilar: Prime Time Love*. I'm sure it was a really amazing show.
- Carlton Fisk is still annoyed with Deion Sanders.

SANDERS'S DOUBLE LIFE

NATIONAL FOOTBALL LEAGUE	MAJOR LEAGUE BASEBALL
Atlanta Falcons (1989–1993)	New York Yankees (1989–1990)
San Francisco 49ers (1994)	Atlanta Braves (1991–1994)
Dallas Cowboys (1995–1999)	Cincinnati Reds (1994–1995)
Washington Redskins (2000)	San Francisco Giants (1995)
Baltimore Ravens (2004–2005)	Cincinnati Reds (1997, 2001)

ROY SULLIVAN

BORN IN GREENE COUNTY, VA • DIED IN DOOMS, VA • 1912–1983

Occasionally, in order to be extraordinary you need to do nothing more than exist . . . to be in the right place at the right time. In the case of Roy Sullivan, it was more about being in the *wrong* place at the *wrong* time. During the course of his life, he was struck by lightning *seven* times! *Ouch.*

The odds of getting struck by lightning just once are estimated at about one in ten thousand. In other words, it's extremely rare. The odds of getting struck by lightning *seven* times would be that number multiplied by itself seven times—far more zeros than I feel like writing on this page.

Sullivan's odds were perhaps a bit higher since he spent much of his life outdoors, working as a park ranger in Shenandoah National Park in Virginia. (Virginia averages thirty-five to forty-five thunderstorms a year, mostly in June, July, and August.)

Nonetheless, for unknown reasons, Sullivan seemed to act as a magnet to lightning. By the fourth strike, he began wondering if some force was trying to destroy him. Thunderstorms would make him very nervous (for good reason). If he happened to be driving when a storm blew through, he would pull over and lie down on the seat until it passed. He also began carrying a can of water in his vehicle to douse any fire caused by the lightning.

Sadly, people often avoided him later in life fearing that they'd also be hit. Sullivan questioned his bad luck. "Why me?" he would ask, while raising his eyes to the sky. Nonetheless, he survived all seven lightning strikes. He passed away at the age of seventy-one in Dooms, Virginia. Yes, that's the actual name of the town.

ROY SULLIVAN WAS STRUCK BY LIGHTNING
SEVEN TIMES!

All seven strikes were documented by the superintendent of Shenandoah National Park and verified by doctors.

STRIKE 1 (1942) — While sitting in a fire lookout tower. "It must have come through the ceiling. It knocked me over, chair and all."

STRIKE 2 (1969) — While driving. "It came through the window and it got me on the right side of the head and I was knocked unconscious." It burned off his eyebrows, eyelashes, and most of his hair. His truck nearly rolled off a cliff edge.

STRIKE 3 (1970) — Lightning struck a power transformer near his home and then bounced to his shoulder. "I had just walked out of the trailer, and was standing nearby when it came down and hit me on the shoulder and it rolled me over and onto the ground."

STRIKE 4 (1972) — In a ranger station. It set his hair on fire. He used a wet towel to put out the fire.

STRIKE 5 (1973) — While on patrol, he noticed a cloud that seemed to be following him. He tried to outrun it, and when he thought he had, he stepped out of the truck, and was struck by a lightning bolt. Again, it set his hair on fire, and also knocked off one of his shoes (without untying it).

STRIKE 6 (1976) — While walking by a creek in a meadow. "It got me right on the hip and it came out by my big toe."

STRIKE 7 (1977) — While sitting on a rock, fishing. "The darn thing came along and hit me on the head and I fell off into the creek." It burned his chest and stomach.

INCIDENTALLY
Sullivan's wife was also struck once when she and Roy were in the backyard hanging clothes.

NIKOLA TESLA

BORN IN SMILJAN, AUSTRIAN EMPIRE (NOW CROATIA) • DIED IN NEW YORK, NY • 1856–1943

Sure, Thomas Edison gets all the glory for inventing the lightbulb (which, incidentally, he didn't actually invent; he just came up with a practical commercial version), but thanks to his former employee and lifelong nemesis, Nikola Tesla, all those bulbs were actually lit! Tesla's advances to alternating current (AC) power (versus Edison's direct current [DC] power) made it possible for us to efficiently provide electricity, not just to lightbulbs but to every appliance in our homes today.

And if that's not enough to convince you of Tesla's awesomeness, he also held at least 275 patents, and was a pioneer in discovering and developing X-ray technology, laser technology, fluorescent lighting, wireless communication, cellular communication, radar, and remote controls.

Unfortunately, Tesla was not the best businessman and had a hard time commercializing his work. Because of this, those who followed in his footsteps often received credit for Tesla's discoveries, and he died alone in New York City with very little money to his name. Compared to Edison, Tesla is often just a footnote in the history books. Herewith, I present a spread on the extraordinary genius that was Nikola Tesla . . .

TESLA COIL

One of his most famous inventions, the Tesla coil, is a high-frequency transformer that can take a regular 120-volt output and step it up to well above a million volts. The voltage is then discharged in the form of electrical arcs (i.e., mini lightning bolts), which you've probably seen in movies such as *Frankenstein*.

Tesla coils were primarily used for radio transmitters and wireless telegraphy. They are also supercool because they create powerful electrical fields, which can be used to wirelessly light fluorescent bulbs up to 50 feet (15.2 metres) away. Astonishingly, even burned-out fluorescent lights will glow.

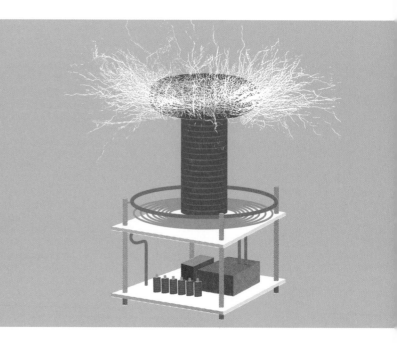

WAR OF THE CURRENTS

Thomas Edison was determined to sell his direct-current system to the nation. The only problem was that Tesla's alternating-current system stood in the way. Edison fought hard against Tesla (as well as against George Westinghouse, who had purchased Tesla's patent), stating that the AC system was too dangerous. Edison's DC system, however, couldn't travel farther than two miles without making a pit stop at a power plant. Tesla's system could travel hundreds of miles, use thinner wire, and transmit higher voltages—and therefore ultimately won the battle.

MARCONI BOLONEY?

Guglielmo Marconi has generally been credited with inventing the radio. He even received the Nobel Prize in Physics after successfully sending the first transatlantic message. But guess what? Everything he did was based on work that had already been done by Tesla. When Tesla was questioned about Marconi's success, his response was, "Marconi is a good fellow. Let him continue. He is using seventeen of my patents."

HELEN THAYER

In 1986, at the age of fifty, New Zealand–born explorer Helen Thayer became the first woman and the oldest person to travel solo to the North Magnetic Pole. She pulled her own sled, which weighed 160 pounds (72.5 kilograms), and didn't make any stops for resupply.

Thayer's trek, which took nearly a month, traveled through areas heavily populated by hungry polar bears. Toward the end of her journey, a storm blew away most of her food, leaving her with only five walnuts and 1 pint (473 millilitres) of water for each day. But guess what? She made it!

Since then, Thayer has walked across the Sahara desert following an ancient trade route (a 4,000-mile [6,437-kilometre] journey); kayaked 2,200 miles (3,541 kilometres) along the Amazon River; and even lived alongside a wolf den in the Canadian Arctic for more than six months to study wild wolves in their environment.

In 2002 Thayer was named "One of the Great Explorers of the 20th Century" by *National Geographic*, and was honored by the White House and the National Geographic Society. Today, she continues her exploration of some of the most remote places on the planet, and then shares her adventures with audiences around the world.

THAYER'S TWENTY-SEVEN-DAY JOURNEY TO THE NORTH MAGNETIC POLE

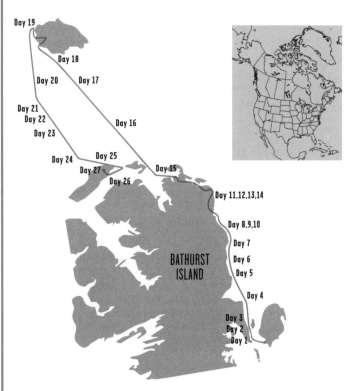

Note: The North Magnetic Pole, where our compasses point, is not to be confused with the Terrestrial North Pole, which is the northern axis on which Earth spins. Just in case you were wondering.

A RIDICULOUSLY EASY MULTIPLE-CHOICE QUIZ

1. In addition to being a great explorer, Helen Thayer is also . . .
   a) an accomplished high-altitude climber.
   b) a United States National luge champion.
   c) one of the top discus throwers in America, with a personal best of 204 feet (62 metres).
   d) all of the above.
2. In addition to being all of the above, Helen Thayer is also . . .
   a) a photographer who captured pictures of three animal species in the Amazon previously unknown to scientists.
   b) an internationally acclaimed motivational speaker.
   c) a bestselling author of three books.
   d) all of the above.

Although Thayer's dog, Charlie, is not a person, he still deserves credit for being extraordinary. The 94-pound (42.6-kilogram) Husky mix traveled with her to the North Pole, helping to keep her safe from bears. Helen also took Charlie with her to live alongside the wolf pack, letting him act as a go-between—after all, he was the great-great-grandson of an arctic gray wolf.

Answers: 1. (d); 2. (d).

LÉON THEREMIN

BORN IN SAINT PETERSBURG, RUSSIA • DIED IN MOSCOW, RUSSIA • 1896–1993

Léon Theremin (or Lev Termen to the Russians) is the inventor of the theremin, one of the strangest and most fascinating musical instruments ever conceived. It's played without ever actually being touched! You move your hands in proximity to two metal antennas, one controlling pitch and the other controlling volume. The sound is somewhat eerie, and often described as a female voice, or perhaps a warbling cello. You've probably heard the theremin in old horror or sci-fi films, but it can also make beautiful melodies when played by an accomplished performer.

The story of Léon Theremin is just as extraordinary as the musical instrument he created. He grew up in Saint Petersburg, Russia, where he had an early fascination with electricity and physics. By the time he was in high school, he had his own laboratory, and at the age of twenty-four, while experimenting with high-frequency oscillators, he invented a new musical instrument. He called it the Termenvox, though it would eventually come to be known as the theremin. He had the opportunity to demonstrate it to Russian leader Vladimir Lenin, who was so impressed that he sent Theremin to the United States to demonstrate the invention . . . and to spy on other engineers!

For eleven years, Theremin lived in America, where he promoted his instrument, patented it, and even struck a manufacturing deal with Radio Corporation of America for mass assembly. He also taught lessons, taking on one particularly talented student named Clara Rockmore. She played the theremin like no one had before, masterfully and with haunting elegance. In fact, the playing methods and finger techniques Rockmore developed are still used to this day. Theremin was smitten with Rockmore, and even proposed to her, though she went on to marry another man.

Some speculate that during his time in the United States, Theremin also hobnobbed with many other inventors, gaining access to top-secret information he would relay back to the Soviet government.

In 1938 Theremin mysteriously disappeared. It is unclear whether he returned to Russia by choice, or if he was forced to do so by Russian secret police. What is known is that he ended up in a *sharashka*, or work camp, where he was forced to create equipment for the government. In particular, he is credited with inventing "The Thing," a secret listening device that was used to spy on private conversations held in the U.S. ambassador's office in Moscow.

Ultimately, after many years of working for the secret police, Theremin was released, and immediately went back to working on his musical instrument. The remainder of his life was largely devoted to building theremins and teaching the instrument at the Moscow Conservatory of Music. In 1991 he returned to the United States, where he was briefly reunited with Rockmore.

Léon Theremin lived to be ninety-seven. Today, the theremin is mass-produced by Moog Music; its most popular version of the instrument, the Etherwave, has sold more than 30,000 since 1996. In fact, I own one.

Clara Rockmore, also a Russian émigré, worked very closely with Theremin during his time in the United States. She quickly became his protégée, and is considered to be one of the best thereminists to have lived. You should check out some of her music right this very second!

SO, HOW DOES IT WORK?

The closer your hand gets to the vertical antenna, the higher the pitch. The closer your hand gets to the horizontal antenna, the quieter the volume. The movement of the player's hands are meant to evoke those of a conductor's.

TRUE OR TRUE?

1. Theremin performed with the New York Philharmonic.
2. Theremin's grandniece, Lydia Kavina, is considered one of the world's top performers of the theremin.
3. Theremin also invented the Rhythmicon, the world's first electronic drum machine.
4. The theremin was the first electronic musical instrument to be mass-produced.
5. Theremin also invented a platform that could convert dance movements into sounds.

Answers: 1. T; 2. T; 3. T; 4. T; 5. T.

MARK TWAIN

BORN IN FLORIDA, MO • DIED IN REDDING, CT • 1835–1910

When it comes to extraordinary writers, few can top Mark Twain . . . and not only because of his awesome mustache and white suit.

Mark Twain, born Samuel Clemens, was a witty intellectual best known for his novels *The Adventures of Tom Sawyer* and *Adventures of Huckleberry Finn*. His colorful life, however, extends far beyond that—he was also a journalist, inventor, lecturer, and even a riverboat pilot!

Twain was born in 1835, as Halley's Comet passed Earth. Twain would later predict that he would "go out" when the comet returned, an occurrence that takes place every seventy-five to seventy-six years.

As a young man, he worked for a small newspaper owned by his brother. He would often contribute articles and humorous sketches. During a trip down the Mississippi to visit New Orleans, a steamboat pilot helped convince Twain that he, too, should become a pilot. And he did!

Twain had the time of his life navigating boats on the Mississippi, at least until the Civil War broke out. After a mere two weeks as a volunteer Confederate soldier (and having seen no military action), he headed west to San Francisco to restart his journalistic career. He also began publishing narratives, many of which became successful.

But it wasn't until Twain married, had kids, and moved to Connecticut that he made his big splashes with *Tom Sawyer* and its sequel *Huckleberry Finn*. In these books he was able to capture the dialect of people along the Mississippi in a way that had never been done before. But more important was his ability to shine a light on a world shadowed by racism. Meanwhile, Twain started a publishing house, printing such books as a memoir by former president Ulysses S. Grant. Unfortunately, his publishing business didn't do so well, and he eventually went bankrupt.

Twain continued writing, and even began touring (wearing only white suits) to help pay off his debts, all the while becoming more famous. Along the way he befriended such greats as Nikola Tesla, Helen Keller, and Thomas Edison.

Throughout the course of his career, Twain published dozens of books as well as numerous stories, lectures, and essays. In the last fifteen years of his life, he had become one of the most celebrated writers in the world.

In 1910, at the age of seventy-four, Mark Twain died in his Connecticut home, as Halley's Comet passed Earth once again.

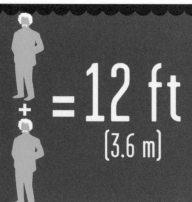

= 12 ft (3.6 m)

JUST HOW DEEP IS MARK TWAIN?

Mark Twain's real name was Samuel Langhorne Clemens. His pen name, "Mark Twain," came from his years working on Mississippi riverboats. "Twain" is an old word meaning "two." A riverboatman would drop a line into the water to measure its depth, making sure it was deep enough for the boat to pass. If the line dropped all the way to the second mark, then he would call out, "Mark twain!" Each "twain" equals 6 feet (1.8 metres). Therefore the depth at mark twain is 12 feet (3.6 metres). Mark Twain, the writer, however, was less than 6 feet (1.8 metres) tall.

WHICH ANSWER IS TOTALLY ABSURD?

1. Mark Twain loved science. He patented several inventions including . . .
   a) mustache wax made from peanut oil.
   b) a self-pasting scrapbook.
   c) a trivia game called Memory Builder.
   d) adjustable straps to replace suspenders.

2. Mark Twain once said . . .
   a) "If you tell the truth, you don't have to remember anything."
   b) "Man is the only animal that blushes, or needs to."
   c) "It is better to deserve honors and not have them than to have them and not deserve them."
   d) "I see a little silhouetto of a man, Scaramouche, Scaramouche will you do the fandango?"

RUTH WAKEFIELD

BORN IN EAST WALPOLE, MA • DIED IN DUXBURY, MA • 1903–1977

It's hard to believe there was a time before chocolate chip cookies. And what an unfortunate time it must have been. Thankfully, Ruth Wakefield, a Massachusetts inn-keeper, changed the history of cookies for the better.

In 1930 Ruth and her husband, Kenneth, purchased a former toll house (basically the equivalent of a truck stop for horse-drawn carriages) near Whitman, Massachusetts, and turned it into an inn.

Ruth spent a great deal of her time baking for guests. On one particular day, while attempting to make a batch of very basic butter cookies, she chopped a bar of chocolate into small pieces and added them to the dough, expecting them to melt. To her surprise, the chips kept their shape, helping create what would become one of the most beloved cookies of all time. Word spread among her guests, and eventually the recipe was published in several New England newspapers.

Within a few years, Ruth had struck a deal with Nestlé, and the recipe for her "Toll House Cookies" was printed on the wrapper of every bar of semisweet chocolate. As the popularity of the chocolate chip cookie grew, Nestlé and other companies began making their own packaged chocolate morsels. Of course, now you can simply buy a box of premade chocolate chip cookies, but I'm guessing (just guessing) that they're not quite as good as Ruth Wakefield's.

ANSWER BOTH QUESTIONS CORRECTLY, AND WIN A CHOCOLATE CHIP COOKIE!

(FINE PRINT: YOU ALSO HAVE TO MAKE THE COOKIES IN ORDER TO WIN THE COOKIE.)

1. Ruth Graves Wakefield's cookbook, *Toll House Tried and True Recipes* . . .
   a) was a huge success, and sold millions of copies.
   b) was a complete flop, and can now only be found in historic toll houses throughout Massachusetts.
   c) also contained a recipe for Toll House Fruit Mallow Biscuits.
   d) was illegible, because it was covered in chocolate.

2. For Ruth's recipe, Nestlé paid her . . .
   a) $1,000,000.
   b) a lifetime supply of chocolate.
   c) $375.
   d) a chocolate Labrador retriever puppy.

Answers: 1. (a) and (c), though I'm still not sure what a "fruit mallow biscuit" is!? 2. (b) a lifetime supply of chocolate. Booyah!

LARRY WALTERS

BORN IN LOS ANGELES, CA • DIED IN LOS ANGELES, CA • 1949–1993

Up, up, and away! Ever since humans have existed we have fantasized about flying. Even now, after a century of airplanes, helicopters, and rocket ships that have taken us to the moon, we still have these dreams. At least *I* do.

Apparently, so did Larry Walters, a thirty-three-year-old truck driver from Los Angeles, California, who, on July 2, 1982, strapped himself into an aluminum lawn chair and lifted into the sky with the help of forty-five helium-filled weather balloons. It couldn't have been a more fantastic and basic flying machine. He carried sandwiches, a bottle of soda, a camera, a CB radio, and a BB gun so that he could pop balloons for his descent.

"Lawnchair Larry," as he became known, soared into the sky like an elevator to an altitude of 16,000 feet (4.9 kilometres)—that's eleven times higher than the Empire State Building)—and floated for ninety minutes. His twenty-year dream had finally come true! (Well, sort of.)

Although Walters had hoped to leisurely float toward the Mojave Desert, he ended up drifting to a much higher altitude than anticipated. Cold, frightened, and dangerously close to commercial jets approaching the Long Beach Airport, he radioed air traffic controllers to alert them of his presence. He then shot several of the balloons to begin his descent.

As Walters lowered onto a Long Beach neighborhood, police saw that he was approaching power lines and quickly shut off the electricity. Amazingly, after a brief entanglement, he climbed to the ground, unharmed, 15 miles (24 kilometres) from his liftoff point. Lawnchair Larry!

INCIDENTALLY

- He wore a parachute, just in case.
- The Federal Aviation Administration (FAA) fined him $1,500 for air traffic violations.
- Walters called his flying machine *Inspiration I*.
- According to the Associated Press: "A United pilot first spotted Larry. He radioed the tower and described passing a guy in a lawn chair . . . with a gun!"
- Although Larry brought a camera, he was so amazed by the view that he didn't take a single picture.
- After shooting a couple balloons, Larry accidentally dropped the BB gun overboard. Oops.
- His entanglement with the power lines caused a twenty-minute blackout in a Long Beach neighborhood.
- After the flight, Larry said, "Since I was thirteen years old, I've dreamed of going up into the clear blue sky in a weather balloon. By the grace of God, I fulfilled my dream. But I wouldn't do this again for anything."

And here's that stamp of

In case it's not obvious, Walters's stunt was foolishly dangerous and should not be replicated. Instead, maybe save up your money and go for a ride in a professionally piloted hot air balloon.

MALALA YOUSAFZAI

Malala Yousafzai simply wanted to go to school, like most other eleven-year-old girls around the world. Maybe one day she would even become a doctor! Unfortunately, a militant group known as the Taliban had taken over the once-peaceful Swat Valley in Pakistan where Malala lived. Because of the Taliban's strict religious beliefs, they decided that girls should not be allowed to get an education. In fact, they had blown up more than a hundred girls' schools in the area. Those who defy the rules of the Taliban are punished or even killed.

Malala kept a blog for the BBC (British Broadcasting Corporation) describing her life under Taliban rule. Soon after, a *New York Times* reporter flew to Pakistan to interview Malala and document her story. Her reputation as an incredibly brave girl quickly grew throughout the Western world.

Back home, however, the Taliban saw Malala as a threat. One day while she was riding the bus home from school, a Taliban gunman boarded the bus and shot her in the head. By a miracle, she survived.

Since the assassination attempt, Malala Yousafzai has changed her mind. She no longer wants to become a doctor; she now wants to become a politician, so that she can fight for her country. In her own words: "Swat Valley! *Zindabad!*" (That means *Long live Swat Valley!*) In my own words: "Malala Yousafzai! *Zindabad!*"

SIX POINTS OF AWESOMENESS FOR MALALA

1. In 2013 Malala Yousafzai became the youngest person in history to be nominated for a Nobel Peace Prize.

2. When she was just twelve, Malala met with Richard Holbrooke, President Barack Obama's top official in Pakistan, and said, "Respected ambassador, if you can help us in our education, so please help us."

3. November 10 has been designated by U.N. Secretary-General Ban Ki-moon as Malala Day! (The date falls one month after when she was shot.)

4. The name Malala means "grief stricken." She was named after Malalai of Maiwand, an Afghan poet and warrior woman.

5. The singer Madonna dedicated her song "Human Nature" to Malala at a 2012 concert in Los Angeles.

6. Former British Prime Minister Gordon Brown came up with the slogan "I Am Malala" to help petition for all children worldwide to be in school by 2015.

A FEW CLOSING WORDS

SO, YOU STILL THINK YOU'RE EXTRAORDINARY?

Tell me about it. E-mail me at info@michaelhearst.com.
While you're at it, check out some of my other projects at Michaelhearst.com.

MEGA THANKS TO:

Joe Beshenkovsky, Jason Bitner, Linsey Bostwick, Terry Byer, Olivier Conan, Luis Cruz, Betsy Eudailey, Forrest Eudailey, Claudia Gonson, Alex Graf, Dan Graf, Tatiana Graf, Temple Grandin, Jesse Hardman, Ryan Hayes, Benjamin Hearst, Jeanie Hearst, Earl Hearst, Nathan Hearst, Ben Holmes, Brigid Hughes, ICareIfYouListen.com, Kazuki Ishizaki, Katinka Israël, Raphaël Israël, Yonatan Israël, Christy Jaramillo, William Kamkwamba, Jud Laghi, Allyssa Lamb, Fiona Maazel, Melissa Manlove, John McQeeney, Steve Mockus, Moog Inc., Kristin Mueller, Rodney Mullen, Ronit Muszkatblit, Park Slope Public Library, Alan Rapp, Mary Roach, Alain Robert, Yuya Saito, Aaron Lewis Scamihorn, Helen Thayer, Dawn Vincent, Peter Wright, everyone at Barbès, everyone at Colson Patisserie, and everyone at Chronicle Books.

ABOUT THE AUTHOR

MICHAEL HEARST is a musician and a writer. He is the author of the book *Unusual Creatures*, and of course the one that you are holding in your hand. As a musician, he has recorded and released over a dozen albums, some with his band, One Ring Zero, others under his own name, such as *Songs for Ice Cream Trucks*, *Songs for Unusual Creatures*, and *Songs for Fearful Flyers*. He has also composed music for several films, most recently *Magic Camp* and *To Be Takei*. Hearst lives in Brooklyn, New York, in a smallish third-floor apartment. Thankfully, there are grapevines outside his window.

ABOUT THE ILLUSTRATOR

AARON SCAMIHORN is an artist from Indianapolis, Indiana. He designs, illustrates, and hand screen prints gig posters for bands such as Arctic Monkeys, Cake, and Queens of the Stone Age.
You can see more of his work online at Ronlewhorn.com.